Gastronomical Barbecue Cookbook

Ann

Published by

 GENERAL STORE
PUBLISHING HOUSE

I Main Street, Burnstown, Ontario, Canada K0J IG0
Telephone 1-800-465-6072 Fax 613-432-7184

ISBN 1-896182-35-6
Printed and bound in Canada

Layout and Design by Leanne Enright

General Store Publishing House gratefully acknowledges the assistance
of the Ontario arts Council and Canada Council.

Canadian Cataloguing in Publication Data

Campbell, Ann, 1948-
  The gastronomical barbecue cookbook

ISBN 1-896182-35-6

1. Barbecue cookery. I. Title.

TX840.B3C35 1995 641.7'6 C95-900414-9

First Printing March 1996

Open Letter

We would like to take this opportunity to thank you for selecting BROILMASTER! and to express our confidence that it will live up to your every expectation.

We, and the publisher of this cookbook, who has many years and a vast range of experience in developing gas barbecue cookbooks, have collaborated to come up with this **Gastronomical Barbecue Cookbook.** We hope it helps refine your skills and inspires you to create culinary masterpieces . . . after all, anything you can cook indoors with your oven or range can be cooked outdoors with your BROILMASTER

Our thanks to you, once again, and our thanks, too, to the publisher for their time in developing this BROILMASTER Cookbook.

BROILMASTER

TABLE OF CONTENTS

MEAT

FISH

SEAFOOD

Understanding Your
Broilmaster® Gas Grill

Your ownership of a BROILMASTER Gas Grill opens the door to a new outdoor cooking experience.

It is likely that much of the cooking formerly done with your range and oven in the kitchen will now be done outdoors on your BROILMASTER. Why? Because this gas grill, with its adjustable flame control and wide range of cooking temperatures, has almost unlimited versatility. It can be used for surface cooking or rotisserie cooking. It grills, bakes, or cooks by a combination of the three. Perhaps most important of all . . . meats, fish, fowl and other foods grilled on BROILMASTER have that wonderful, tangy, smoky flavor formerly associated with charcoal grilling and open pit barbecuing.

"Charcoal Flavor" Without Charcoal?

The now widely recognized truth is charcoal is odorless and flavorless. If you have ever lit a charcoal fire, you know it burns without smoke or aroma until you start cooking. The so-called "charcoal flavor" is imparted to the meat or food by the smoke and flames resulting from the dripping of juices on the hot coals. A gas grill creates this same delicious, smoky flavor by the same process. Instead of charcoal, chunks of naturally cured clay briquets are heated in the gas flames to provide the hot coals.

Your Broilmaster® Gives You Complete Cooking Control

If you have been using a charcoal grill for your outdoor cooking in the past, you will probably go through a short period of "getting used to" your gas grill. But you will soon find that your gas grill offers several important advantages. You not only avoid the work, expense and mess of charcoal, but you gain much more accurate control of cooking results. In any model of BROILMASTER, you can accurately control cooking temperatures, for any length of time, by one or more of these methods.

1. Adjusting the gas burner valve to any setting between HI and LO (infinite adjustment).

2. Lowering the grill lid to one of three heights above the cooking surface or closing completely (for maximum cooking temperature).

3. Positioning the cooking grids at different levels or angles above the "Charmaster" clay briquets.

4. Changing the low flame setting.

Basic Operating Instructions

1. Initial Lighting

The burner lighting procedure is basically the same for all models of BROILMASTER® outdoor gas grills. Follow igniter lighting instruction on grill if present, or these instructions:

   (a) With grill lid open, insert lighted safety match (the kind with wooden stick—not a paper match) through the lighter hole.

   (b) Making certain match is still burning inside grill, push in and turn knob counterclockwise to "HI" setting. Burner should ignite. If not, wait 5 minutes before repeating above procedures.

NOTE! If you find grill difficult to light because of strong or gusty winds, partially close grill lid before inserting lighted match.

2. Preheating Grill

Before cooking, always preheat the grill a few minutes on "HI" burner setting with the lid closed. This gives the "Charmaster" clay briquets time to heat up in the gas flames. Hot coals mean better, quicker cooking and better flavor.

Caution: Don't leave the grill operating on "HI" burner setting and the lid closed for longer than 30 minutes.

If you are not ready to cook after preheating the grill, raise the lid and use a lower burner setting.

3. Positioning the Cooking Grids

The cooking grids in most BROILMASTER Gas Grills may be placed in both level and tilted positions.

The tilt positions are used mainly for the purpose of draining grease faster into a grease receptacle when cooking meats of high fat content.

The lowest level grid position will accommodate quick searing without cooking meats throughout, for "rare" degree of doneness. Higher levels of cooking grids allow for slower cooking, for more "well-done" dishes.

Various Ways To Cook
With Your Broilmaster®

1. Surface grilling with lid raised.

This method of grilling exposes only the bottom of the meat or food to cooking temperatures. It is the slowest method of cooking on a gas grill, and is therefore suitable only for foods that cook quickly—like bacon, hot dogs, fish fillets, thin steaks or chops, hors d'oeuvres, shish-kabobs, etc.

People who don't particulary care for a smoky flavor may prefer this method because it provides the least "barbecue" taste. For obvious reasons, it is not a good method when the weather is cold or windy.

2. Surface grilling with lid lowered (or closed completely)

There's no question—you get more flavor when you grill or cook with the lid of your BROILMASTER Gas Grill lowered or closed completely. Therefore, this is by far the most popular method of cooking among BROILMASTER users.

Meats and foods cook more quickly when the lid is lowered, because heat is confined in the grill and both the top and bottom surfaces of the meat or food are exposed to cooking temperatures.

You get more flaming and more smoke, and therefore more smoky flavor—but you have to be careful, or you will over-char and over-cook the food. When grilling hamburgers or steaks, most users will use the HI burner setting—particularly if they like their meat rare or medium. This method insures quick searing and charring of the outside surface without overcooking the center of the meat.

Your own experience will quickly acquaint you with this method of cooking, so you will know what burner settings will produce the cooking results you want, and whether to close the lid completely or prop it open a bit.

3. Roasting, Baking or Barbecuing

By closing the lid of your BROILMASTER Gas Grill you can also make it an oven. By means of burner adjustment and the heat indicator, you can control the temperature inside the grill and use it to bake, roast or barbecue a great variety of foods. For example, you can bake potatoes and vegetables in the closed grill, and then keep the potatoes hot on the warming rack while grilling the steaks, hamburgers or whatever!

4. Hugga-Rack/Rotisserie Grilling

The most popular accessory for BROILMASTER Gas Grill is the patented Deluxe "Hugga-Rack."™

It comes complete with Hugga-Grids (that can handle whole turkeys and hams) and a flat basket (great for fish and chicken pieces). A standard rotisserie is available for each Broilmaster. Either makes rotisserie grilling on your BROILMASTER a great cooking method and offers the following advantages:

1. Meats brown and cook evenly on all exposed surfaces.

2. Rotisserie-grilled foods do not require constant attention.

3. Whole turkeys, hams, large roasts can be cooked or barbecued with delicious results.

4. Exact degree of doneness can be easily determined by use of a meat thermometer.

Whether to rotisserie grill with the grill lid raised or lowered?

Meats cooked on a Hugga-Rack or rotisserie with a lower burner setting and the grill lid lowered, will usually be more tender and have a more smoky flavor. This method of cooking exposes the meat to a combination of grilling and baking. It is an outstanding and flavorful way to cook meat and fowl!

5. Closed Lid Grilling or Baking

Many outdoor cooking enthusiasts use this method most of the time. They like the smoke and flames and the extra smoky flavor it produces.

Many backyard chefs grill steaks (preferably thick), chops and hamburgers with the burner on "HI" setting and grill lid completely closed.

This method produces quicker cooking, smoky flavor and more browning of the meat. It is particulary effective in preparing rare steaks or chops, because it quickly sears and browns the outside of the meat while leaving the inside appetizingly rare.

For slower cooking the burner should be at a lower setting. A combination of a lower burner setting and partially raising the lid will produce cooking temperatures in the 300 to 400 degrees level needed for slow cooking or grilling. Slow cooking insures maximum tenderness and less shrinkage of all kinds of meat and fowl.

Used as an oven, your BROILMASTER Gas Grill achieves marvellous baking results. It's great for roasting foil-wrapped corn on the cob, vegetables of all sorts, potatoes, or prepare any "main course" that would heat up your kitchen and make your air conditioner work harder!

6. Indirect "Convection" Cooking

Light just one side of your twin burner and place chicken pieces, ham, turkey, etc on the grids over the unfired side. This will "bake" the dish without any flare-up.Use this method to bake cakes, pies, breads and cookies, or vegetables . . . any dish into which you don't want an outdoor, smoky flavor imparted.

STEAK

Only BROILMASTER® offers up to three different grilling levels that allow you to grill rare, medium and well done steak at the same time.

If your BROILMASTER Gas Grill was used for no other purpose than to grill STEAK, it would be worth every cent you paid for it! Steaks grilled outdoors over the "Charmaster" clay briquets of your BROILMASTER have a flavor unsurpassed by any other cooking method.

Best Choices for Grilling

For best results choose Sirloin, T-Bone, Porterhouse, Filet Mignon (tenderloin), Club, Ribeye, and preferred grades are Prime and Choice.

For great grilling, a steak should be from 1 1/2 to 2 inches thick. 1-inch thickness is minimum. A thin steak quickly becomes overdone and dried out, and loses much of its taste appeal.

Tips For Grilling Steaks

1. Remove steaks from refrigerator 1 to 2 hours before cooking.

2. Trim off excess fat and suet, leaving a thin edge of fat. Score the fat to prevent curling during cooking.

3. Rub salad oil on cooking rack to minimize sticking.

4. Do not salt meat while cooking; salt draws out juices and increases flare-up.

5. Turn steaks with tongs or spatula. Piercing meat with a fork releases juices and increases flare-up.

6. Use higher burner settings and a low grid position for rare steak, and lower burner settings and higher grid position for medium and well-doneness.

7. To increase smoky flavor, lower lid to one of three positions provided by the lid stop located on the left side of the grill, or close cover completely.

8. Generally, the most flavorful method is achieved by grilling steaks with the burner on HI setting and the grill lid closed.

9. Do not leave steaks unattended. For the most delicious and appetizing steaks, be johnny-on-the-spot to turn and remove them from the grill just at the right time!

10. Like that "smoked" taste? For best results use one of BROIL-MASTER'S "Smoker" Accessories or sprinkle dampened wood chips on the "Charmaster" clay briquets a few minutes before steaks are done and lower lid. The result—truly smoked flavor!

PORK

Grilled, baked or barbecued on a BROILMASTER® Gas Grill, pork becomes delicious and nutritious food.

Consider these delectable pork possibilities—3/4 to 1inch thick blade steaks country-style; back ribs; spare ribs; shoulder roast; loin roast; smoked ham; smoked ham slices; kabobs; ground pork; tenderloin; Canadian style bacon; sausage . . . to mention a few cuts. Choose the leaner, meatier cuts of fresh pork and trim off excess fat.

Slow Cooking Best

For a real treat, have your butcher cut some 2-inch thick pork loin chops (the leanest and best he has). Grill them on the grids of your BROILMASTER, with the burner at a medium or low setting and the grill lid closed or partially closed. Place grids at a high level.

Season the chops to your liking and turn the chops every 10 or 15 minutes to insure even cooking. (Use a spatula or tongs . . . not a fork).

The pork chops should be done in 45 minutes to an hour (if you have resisted the impulse to speed up cooking).

Today's pork is leaner, meatier and more tender. All fresh pork roasts should be cooked to an internal temperature of 170 degrees F. for the most juicy, tender and flavorful roast. The meat thermometer should register 160 degrees F. for "cook-before-eating" hams, and 140 degrees F. for "fully-cooked" hams.

Pork roasts vary in shape, size, amount of bone, leanness and thickness. A meat thermometer is the most accurate means of determining doneness. Insert meat thermometer with bulb in thickest part, not touching bone.

When using a Hugga-Rack to prepare a roast, insert meat thermometer at a slight angle so tip is in center of roast but not resting on bone. The thermometer must clear the cooking unit while meat is turning.

HAMBURGERS A LA BROILMASTER®

For flavorful hamburgers use a good grade of beef-ground sirloin, round or chuck.

For extra flavor, mix ground onion with the meat, or add hickory smoke seasoning.

Hamburger patties for grilling should be 1/2" to 3/4" thick. Use a HI or MEDIUM burner setting. For a smokier flavor, lower grill lid while cooking.

For rare burgers, use a low grid position. For more well done, use a higher position.

Preheating until the heat indicator reads 400 or 500 degrees is suggested, then place burgers on grids and lower lid. Turn once after 4 to 5 minutes.

Second side will need only about half as much cooking time as the first side. Like cheeseburger? Put a slice of Cheddar cheese or Swiss cheese on each patty after it has been turned and close the grill lid for the final minutes.

No time to watch the burger? Place patties in the Hugga-Rack Flat Basket over a medium flame to 10 to 15 minutes.

If you wish to accumulate hamburger patties, use the warming rack. This will hold the hamburger patties far enough away from the flames to prevent over-cooking, but will keep them at serving temperature.

Helpful Hints for Certain Kinds of Meats, Fish and Fowl

Chicken
HOW TO BROILMASTER® IT!

Chicken ranks high among America's favorite foods. It can be fried, baked, stewed or grilled. It can be seasoned in limitless ways. Yet, what way of cooking makes this domestic fowl more delicious than grilling over an open fire . . . on a BROILMASTER!

Chickens for surface grilling should be fryers or broilers cut in halves or quarters.

1. Surface grilled chicken

    a. Preheat grill at medium burner setting for 10 minutes.

    b. Locate cooking grid at top position. Rub surface of grid with cooking oil to minimize sticking.

    c. Place chicken on grid, cavity side down. The lid may be raised or partially lowered. The chicken will cook faster with the lid lowered.

    d. Turn chicken frequently and baste with melted butter, lemon butter or your favorite basting sauce. If chicken is browning too fast, turn burner knob to lower setting. If you wish, you can baste chicken with a barbecue sauce shortly before cooking is completed. Tomato-based and "sweet" barbecue sauces will burn if exposed to the heat too long.

2. Rotisserie-grilled chicken

Rotisserie-grilled is a favorite way of barbecuing chicken because it cooks the chicken to an appetizing, even brownness and requires less attention. Chicken may be cooked this way with the grill lid lowered to increase the smoky flavor. Whole chickens may be skewered and clamped and tied into position on the rotisserie spit. The spit will hold two average or three small "broiler" type of chickens. Halves and quarters can easily be grilled in the "Hugga-Rack"™ Flat Basket.

Chicken should be brushed occasionally with your favorite basting sauce to keep it moist and tender.

SPARE RIBS

Spare ribs may be completely cooked on the BROILMASTER,® using a "LO" flame-setting and grilling with the lid lowered. However, the ribs will be more tender and juicy if partially baked or steamed first . . . then finished on the grill.

FISH

Fish may be baked in heavy foil—adding lemon slices and seasoning before wrapping securely. Fish steaks and fillets, 3/4 to 1-inch thick, will require about 10 minutes on each side, cooked with lid lowered (not completely closed) and grill preheated on medium flame. The same method may be used with the Hugga-Rack Flat Basket.

TURKEYS

With the Hugga-Rack you may grill a turkey up to 20 lbs. in weight, but better results will be obtained with turkeys of 12 to 16 lbs. weight. Never use a pre-basted turkey! It produces too much grease for satisfactory rotisserie grilling and may catch on fire! The turkey can be placed on the "Hugga"-Grids, stuffed or not, and grilled at low or medium burner setting, with the lid partially lowered. A meat thermometer should be inserted in the breast as a check on doneness.

You may use an indirect method . . . preheat both sides of a twin burner until indicator registers 350-400 degrees then turn off one half of the burner. Load turkey so it will turn over the unfired side. Preheating this side will help brown the turkey to seal in juices. Cook until meat thermometer registers desired temperature and finish off by turning on burner under turkey . . . to firm or even "crisp up" the outermost layer.

KABOBS

Kabobs made of cooked meats, cut in 1 to 1 1/2 inch cubes and skewered, may be cooked over medium heat with lid lowered, turning occasionally until heated through. Uncooked pieces of meat cut in 1-inch cubes and marinated overnight, can be placed on skewers and cooked over medium heat with lid lowered, turning frequently until done. If vegetables and other foods are to be cooked as kabobs, combine on skewer those foods that will cook in about the same length of time. Also be sure that these foods are about the same size.

WHOLE LOBSTERS

Two small whole lobsters, or from six to eight lobster tails can be grilled in the "Hugga-Rack"™ Flat Basket. Brush lobster with melted butter, marinade sauce, or salad oil to keep moist. Cooking time about 20 minutes, or less.

LOBSTER TAILS

Lobster tails can also be surface grilled on the cooking grid with the burner at medium setting. They should be turned frequently to insure even cooking. Brush with melted butter or salad oil to keep moist. Cooking time, about 15 minutes.

Foil-wrapped lobster can be cooked, with or without stuffing, on the grids with the burner on medium setting and the lid lowered. Cooking time, about 15 minutes.

Keeping Your Broilmaster® Gas Grill In Good Operating Condition

At BROILMASTER, we love to barbecue as much as you do and know keeping your grill in good working order is important.

The following suggestions do not require a lot of time or effort to take care of your BROILMASTER.

Some users will clean the interior of the grill frequently, using a brass bristle brush and detergent to clean off the deposits of grease and smoke, because they like that "aluminum" look. The majority of users will allow the aluminum surfaces to darken gradually and will concentrate their cleaning efforts on keeping the cooking grids and exterior surfaces of the grill clean, with an occasional washing of the grill interior. A popular method of gas grill hygiene is burning up the grease and food cinders by leaving the burner on "HI" setting and the lid closed for 15 to 20 minutes after cooking is completed. If you use this "no work" method, don't forget to turn off the burner! If the grill is left burning on HI setting for hours (or days), it could damage the finish and castings.

The burners in BROILMASTER Grills are the most rugged and dependable in the gas grill industry. They are constructed of high quality 430 series stainless steel. However, even this rugged and dependable burner should have an occasional cleaning, particularly if the grill is used often or high-fat meats like pork and spare ribs are frequently cooked on it.

Examine the ports that run continuously around the perimeter of the burner. If grease, rust or food cinders are blocking any of the port area, remove them. Be careful not to drop the burner and crack or damage it.

To clean the outside painted surface of your BROILMASTER, wash occasionally with a mild detergent. The use of the vinyl cover available from your dealer will make the painted finish last longer.

While you are cooking, keep all food preparation surfaces, dishes and utensils clean. Use a clean platter for carrying cooked foods from your BROILMASTER.

SOME SELECTED BROILMASTER® RECIPES

Here are some tested recipes for gas grill cooking furnished by the Home Service Departments of leading gas companies. You can cook almost anything on your BROILMASTER, so don't limit your outdoor cooking experience to these recipes. There are many books on barbecuing and outdoor cooking—for example, the Better Homes & Gardens Barbecue Book—that are a rich source of recipes for foods of all description to cook on your BROILMAS-TER. Also check with your dealer for fine accessories that can help you create "master dishes" outdoors on your grill. Keep all food preparation surfaces, dishes and utensils clean throughout the entire period of time. Use a clean platter for carrying cooked foods from the grill.

Thin, Tangy Barbecue Sauce For Ribs, Brisket or Chicken

I cup ketchup	2 or 3 dashes Tabasco sauce
I cup water	I Tbsp. brown sugar
I tsp. celery	I Tbsp. Worcestershire sauce
1/4 cup wine vinegar	I tsp. salt

Combine all ingredients, heat to boiling and simmer for 30 minutes. Makes enough sauce to baste 4 lbs. of ribs.

Lemon-Herb Sauce

1/3 cup lemon juice	1/4 tsp. dried marjoram
1/4 cup salad oil	1/4 tsp. dried rosemary
2 Tbsp. water	1/4 tsp. dried thyme
1/2 tsp. salt	I small onion, peeled and grated
1/2 tsp. celery salt	I clove garlic, peeled and grated
1/2 tsp. pepper	

In jar with tight fitting lid, combine ingredients. Shake well. Use as marinade before basting sauce during cooking. Makes 3/4 cup sauce.

All-Purpose
Barbecue Sauce

1/2 lb. butter
1 cup honey
1 cup pineapple juice
1 cup lemon juice
1 bottle ketchup
4 oz. can tomato paste
1/2 cup brown sugar

1 tsp. onion salt
1 tsp. green pepper, finely chopped
1 Tbsp. dry mustard
4 dashes Tabasco sauce
1/2 tsp. ground cloves
dash ginger and oregano

Mix together and simmer 30 minutes to blend seasonings. This sauce may be made in advance and stored in refrigerator.

Hot Orange Sauce

1/4 cup hot sauce
1/2 cup orange juice

2 Tbsp. brown sugar
dash garlic powder

Mix all of the ingredients and use to baste chicken or shrimp as you grill.

Easy Beef Marinade

1/2 cup salad oil   I tsp. salt
1/4 cup vinegar   dash pepper
1/4 cup onion, chopped   2 tsp. Worcestershire sauce

Combine all ingredients, mix well. Add steaks, kabobs or roasts and let marinate I to 3 hours.

Steaks and Kabobs Marinade

I 1/2 cups salad oil   3/4 cup soy sauce
1/2 cup wine vinegar   1/4 cup Worcestershire sauce
I 1/2 tsp. dried parsley flakes   2 Tbsp. dry mustard
1/3 cup fresh lemon juice   2 1/4 tsp. salt
2 cloves garlic, crushed (if desired)
Tbsp. coarse, freshly ground black pepper

Combine all ingredients and mix well. Makes about 3 1/2 cups. Marinade can be drained from steaks or chops for a second use. Store tightly covered indefinitely in the freezer, or in the refrigerator for one week.

Tangy Seasoners For Grilled Hamburgers And Steaks

2 tsp. onion, chopped

1/2 tsp. dried basil leaves

1/2 tsp. prepared mustard

2 tsp. snipped chives

1/2 tsp. poultry seasoning

crumbled blue cheese

Melt or whip 1/2 stick margarine or butter and add one of the seasonings. Spoon on meat just before removing from grill to warmer platter.

Grilled Tuna Burger

3 lbs. chopped fresh tuna

5 Tbsp. dijon mustard

1 1/2 cup caramelized onions

8 potato rolls

1/2 cup teriyaki sauce

salt & ground black pepper

3 Tbsp. olive oil

1 cup chicken stock

1 Tbsp. minced ginger

2 tsp. minced garlic

1/2 cup honey

Mix tuna, olive oil and 1 Tbsp. mustard and salt and pepper to taste. Form into eight 6-oz. patties; chill. Bring teriyaki, remaining garlic, chicken stock, ginger and honey to a boil. Simmer until reduced to a thick glaze. Stir in remaining mustard. Grill tuna burgers to medium rare. Warm onions; stir in glaze. Place each burger on a roll, top with onion mixture, and serve.

Grilled Salmon With A Spicy Asian Glaze

6-6 oz. salmon filets

1 cup honey

1 Tbsp. curry powder

2 Tbsp. Nouc Mam (Vietnamese fish sauce)

1 Tbsp. ground cumin

1 Tbsp. Hungarian paprika

1 Tbsp. fresh ground black pepper

Place all of the above ingredients in a non-reactive saucepan. Heat to just below the simmer setting and maintain that temperature for 15 minutes. Pour mixture into bowl and reserve for later use. Grill salmon filets on hot grill, brushing liberally with the glaze as you go. Filets should be cooked until slightly pink in the middle. Be careful not to scorch the glaze or over-cook the fish. Serve immediately.

Lamb Ribs With Shallot - Pepper Butter

1/4 cup white wine

1/4 cup champagne vinegar

1/4 cup shallots, peeled and finely diced

salt to taste

1/4 cup black pepper - coarsely ground

10 oz butter cut into 8 pieces

Shallot Pepper Butter Sauce:

In a small, heavy bottomed, non-reactive sauce pan bring wine, vinegar, shallots, and black pepper to a boil. Maintain a vigorous boil and let the mixture reduce until it thickens and the bubbles start to enlarge. Reduce heat to a low boil and beat in the butter, quickly, using a wire whisk, one piece at a time, being careful not to continue to reduce the mixture as the butter is beaten in. Check the seasoning and add salt as needed. Keep warm until ready to use.

Lamb Riblets:

The day before, place the lamb riblets (uncut) in a non-reactive shallow dish. Sprinkle with some olive oil, black pepper, chopped garlic, and some fresh thyme, rosemary and Italian parsley. Cover and refrigerate overnight.

Over a medium hot fire, grill the riblets. As they cook slowly, sprinkle with some salt. When they are done, let them rest for 5-7 minutes before slicing. Slice them, and arrange on platter, drizzle with some of the sauce. Place additional sauce on the side if you want.

Spicy Grilled Pork Tenderloin Jerk

1 lb. boneless pork tenderloin (chicken may be used as a substitute)

Banana Salsa:

1/4 cup lime juice	5 ripe bananas
1/2 cup diced red onion	1 Tbsp. red wine vinegar
1 cup guava jelly	1 Tbsp. cumin
2 Tbsp. canola or peanut oil	salt and pepper to taste
1 cup orange juice	

Heat oil in saucepan and add onions; cook until soft. Add 3 bananas, mashed, and cook for 5 minutes. Add guava jelly, orange juice, vinegar and cumin; stir and allow to simmer until jelly dissolves. Take mixture off heat and pour into bowl; allow to cool slightly. Add remaining bananas, roughly mashed, along with lime juice and salt and pepper.

Marinade:

1/2 cup chopped scallions	2 Tbsp. dried rosemary
1/3 cup lime juice	1/4 cup fresh thyme, stems removed
1/4 cup orange juice	1 Tbsp. black pepper
1 cup fresh basil leaves	1/4 cup red wine vinegar
1 tsp. salt	2 Tbsp. chopped Italian parsley
1/4 cup dijon mustard	

Combine above ingredients and process into a paste-like mix. Rub each pork tenderloin with the mixture and marinate for at least 2 hours before cooking. Grill pork tenderloin to medium rare and serve with Banana salsa.

The Osteen Family's Sunday Grilled Chicken

2 - 3# chickens, each cut into eight pieces

Marinade:

1/4 cup dijon mustard	1/8 cup freshly ground black pepper
1 cup lemon juice	1/4 cup Inner Beauty hot sauce
1/2 cup freshly chopped herbs of your choice	1/3 cup olive oil
1/4 cup Guldens mustard	

In a non-reactive dish marinate the chicken pieces for at least 2 hours and not more than 4 hours. Grill the chicken pieces over a medium hot fire until just cooked through. Sprinkle the chicken with salt as it cooks.

Grilled Quail With A Bourbon Green Peppercorn Glaze

8 quail, semi-boneless (all bones removed except for wing and leg bones

Glaze
1/2 cup dijon mustard
1/2 cup minced shallots or green onions
1 cup oil (either peanut, olive or walnut)
1 cup canned green peppercorns, drained and slightly crushed
1 Tbsp. tabasco sauce

In a small bowl combine the mustard, egg yolks, and tabasco; whisk to mix. While whisking, slowly add the oil, a tablespoon at a time, until all is incorporated and the sauce is thick. Mix in the rest of the ingredients and put aside.

Marinade:
1/2 cup bourbon
1/3 cup honey

Marinate the quail in the marinade for 8-10 hours. Remove and pat dry. Stir the remaining marinade into the glaze. Brush the quail liberally with the glaze and put on a hot grill. Grill the quail quickly while maintaining high heat. The idea is to end up with a crispy outside and a juicy medium rare inside. Serve immediately.

HORS D'OEUVRES

Tomato Bruschetta

4	tomatoes, chopped	4
2	cloves garlic, peeled and minced	2
1/2 cup	fresh basil, chopped	125 mL
2 tbsp	olive oil	25 mL
	coarsely ground salt and pepper	
	olive oil for grilling	
1 or 2	baguettes	1 or 2

Combine the tomatoes, garlic, basil and olive oil in a bowl and let sit for a half hour or so. Slice the bread in half horizontally and then slice the halves into 3 inch pieces. Brush the slices with olive oil and grill over hot coals until lightly browned on both sides. Spoon the tomato mixture on top and serve. Serves 4, or maybe 6, depending on the size of the loaf of bread.

Basil Toasts

You can make your own infused oils of course, but President's Choice Pure Olive Oil with Basil Essence is excellent for this recipe. To make it yourself, heat a cup of olive oil, add a branch of fresh basil, cool completely and then strain into a sterilized bottle or jar.

I	loaf of crusty bread, at least 9 inches long	I
I/3 cup	olive oil infused with basil leaves	75 mL
I/4 cup	fresh basil, finely chopped	50 mL

Slice the loaf in half horizontally. Cut the halves vertically into three inch pieces. Brush each slice generously with the olive oil and sprinkle with a little basil. Place the bread slices on the grill over moderately hot coals, herb side down. Grill until golden brown. Brush the top of the bread with the olive oil and then turn. Grill until golden brown. Serves 6.

Mushroom Tapenade

Make the tapenade at least a day in advance, when possible. It keeps for five or six days and improves with age. If great bread is unavailable to you, I strongly suggest that you learn to make it. Find yourself a good recipe.

1/3 cup	olive oil	75 mL
1/4 cup	balsamic vinegar	50 mL
2 tbsp	lemon juice	25 mL
I lb	mushrooms	500 g
I cup	black olives packed in oil or brine, drained, pitted and minced	250 mL
3 tbsp	capers, drained and minced	45 mL
4	anchovies, drained and minced	4
3	cloves garlic, minced	3
I	loaf of crusty bread	I

Slice the mushrooms and saute lightly in 2 tablespoons of the olive oil. Cool the mushrooms slightly and mince. Place them in a bowl with the remaining ingredients, except the bread, and mix well. If possible, refrigerate the tapenade for 24 hours. It will keep nicely for a few days.

Slice the loaf of bread in half horizontally and cut the halves into 3 inch pieces. Spoon the tapenade onto the bread and serve. Serves 8.

Chopped Olives on Toast

This dish is only as good as the olives and bread. You can make life easier by throwing the pitted olives in the food processor, but I really like the texture of the minced olives. You can facilitate pitting the olives by crushing them gently with the broad side of a knife first. If you do not have olive oil with garlic essence, rub the bread with a split garlic clove before brushing with olive oil.

2 cups	black and green olives, pitted and minced	500 mL
2 tbsp	capers, minced	25 mL
2 tbsp	extra virgin olive oil	25 mL
1/2 tbsp	fresh rosemary	2 mL
1 tsp	pink peppercorns	5 mL
1	loaf of crusty bread	1
	olive oil with garlic essence for grilling	
4	lemon wedges	4

Combine the olives, capers and olive oil. Crush the rosemary and peppercorns in a mortar and pestle and add to the olive mixture. Cut the loaf of bread in half horizontally and then cut the halves into 4 pieces. Brush the bread with olive oil and grill over moderately hot coals until lightly toasted on either the cut side or both sides. Spoon the olive mixture onto the bread and squeeze a little lemon over top. Serves 4.

Brenda and David's
Barbecued Pheasant

4	boneless pheasant breasts	4
1/3 cup	soya sauce	75 mL
2 tbsp	lemon juice	25 mL
2	cloves garlic, peeled and crushed	2

Cut the pheasant breasts into strips about an inch wide. Combine the soya sauce, lemon juice and garlic in a dish and add the pheasant. Marinate for one hour at room temperature or overnight in the refrigerator. Grill over hot coals, brushing with the marinade and turning once, until the pheasant is nicely browned on the outside and cooked through on the inside. Place on a platter and pass with cocktail napkins. Serves 4 as an hors d'oeuvre.

Jane and Terry's Grilled Peppers and Goat Cheese

2	green peppers	2
2	red peppers	2
2	yellow peppers	2
1/2 lb	goat cheese	250 g
	freshly ground black pepper	
	best quality olive oil	
1/3 cup	fresh herbs, such as basil, or rosemary or a mixture of several kinds, finely chopped	75 mL
	a few sprigs of the same herbs	

Blacken the peppers on all sides, over hot coals. Place in a paper bag to sweat for 10 minutes or so, and then peel the skin from the peppers. Do not wash. Cut the peppers into strips and set aside. Place the goat cheese in an oiled, fire proof, baking dish, drizzle with olive oil, sprinkle with black pepper and fresh herbs and heat over moderate coals with the lid on the barbecue down, until the cheese is heated through. Crumble the cheese into big lumps in the baking dish and add the peppers. Throw a few sprigs of the herbs you are using on the coals of the barbecue. Place the dish back on the barbecue with the lid down until the cheese turns a little golden brown and the peppers are heated through. Serves 6 to 8 as a starter or as a vegetable side dish.

Paul Conway's Smoked Salmon with Basil and Orange

2	thick centre cuts of salmon or 2 salmon fillets	
3 tbsp	kosher or coarse sea salt	45 mL
2 tbsp	sugar	25 mL
	zest of 1 thick-skinned orange	
1 1/2 cups	loosely packed basil leaves	375 mL
1 cup	whipping cream, whipped	250 mL
1 tbsp	honey	15 mL
4 oz	horseradish	100 g

Place the salmon cuts in the freezer for 72 hours. Remove and thaw. Place 1 fillet, skin side down, in the bottom of a dish. Combine the salt and sugar and sprinkle half of it on the salmon. Add half of the zest and half of the basil. Place the other fillet flesh side down on top of the first piece of salmon and add the rest of the salt mixture, zest and basil. Cover with plastic wrap and two heavy cans or bricks. Refrigerate; removing the cans or bricks and basting with the fluid that comes out every day for 3 days. Remove the salmon and scrape away the basil and zest. Save the juice that remains.

If using charcoal, light five coals in a pile. When they are red hot, place them at one end of the grill. Place a small piece of hickory, about the size of your baby finger, on the coals. Put the fish on the grid at the other end of the barbecue.

If you are using a gas barbecue, insert volcanic plates over the lava rocks, light the barbecue on one side and set the piece of hickory on the edge of the lava rocks. Once it ignites, you can turn the grill off or set it at its lowest temperature. Place the salmon on the grid over the unlighted side of the grill.

Close the lid of the barbecue and open the vent over the salmon. Grill or cold smoke for about half an hour. In the meantime, heat the remaining liquid to boiling and then cool to room temperature. Bathe the smoked fish in the sauce to remove the traces of grilling from the fish. Combine the whipped cream and honey and blend well. Fold in the horseradish. Serve with the cold salmon. Serves 6 to 8 as an hors d'oeuvre.

Bill's Chanterelle Risotto

8 cups	of chicken stock, simmering	2 L
6 tbsp	butter	90 mL
2 cups	golden chanterelles, cut in 1/2 inch dice	500 mL
2 cups	arborio superfino rice	500 mL
I	medium onion, chopped	I
3/4 cup	white wine	175 mL
	freshly ground black pepper	
2 tbsp	butter	25 mL
2 tbsp	fresh parsley, finely chopped	25 mL
3/4 cup	Parmigiano Reggiano cheese, freshly grated	175 mL
	black pepper and extra Parmigiano cheese for serving	
4	large chanterelles, cut in half and fried in butter (for garnish)	4

Place the simmering stock on the barbecue over coals just hot enough to keep the stock at a simmer. Place a large pot on the side burner of the gas barbecue, over a moderate flame, and melt the 6 tbsp of butter. Add the onion and cook, stirring with a wooden spoon, until transparent. Add the rice and stir until the rice is coated with butter and translucent. Add the wine and continue to stir, until the wine is almost all absorbed. Start adding the stock, a cup at a time, letting it become absorbed between additions and stirring constantly. When half the stock is gone, add the mushrooms and continue the process. When the rice is soft, just past al dente, turn off the burner and remove it from the heat. Grind on some fresh pepper and add the remaining 2 tbsp of butter, the parsley and parmesan cheese. Stir until well-blended and cover. Let the risotto sit for a minute or two before serving. Serve with extra pepper and Parmigiano Reggiano. Set a piece of fried chanterelle on each serving of risotto. Serves 8 as a starter.

Teriyaki Salmon

1/4 cup	soya sauce	50 mL
1 tbsp	olive oil	15 mL
2	cloves garlic, crushed	2
1 tsp	fresh ginger, grated	5 mL
1 tsp	demerara sugar	5 mL
8	tiny salmon steaks or 8 chunks of salmon	8
	watercress stems	
4	wedges of lemon	4

Combine the soya sauce, olive oil, garlic, ginger and sugar in a dish and add the salmon. Marinate 45 minutes to an hour. Grill over hot coals, brushing with the marinade and turning once, until the steaks are nicely browned and opaque throughout. Place watercress stems in a bouquet on 4 salad plates. Place the steaks on top. Garnish with wedges of lemon. Serves 4.

SALADS

Spring Lamb Salad

I	saddle of lamb trimmed of excess fat	I
3	cloves of garlic, peeled and slivered	3
I/3 cup	olive oil	75 mL
I/4 cup	fresh mint leaves, finely cut	50 mL
3 or 4	bunches fresh watercress	3 or 4
I/3 cup	olive oil	75 mL
3 tbsp	balsamic vinegar	45 mL
I tsp	Dijon mustard	5 mL
I	clove of garlic, crushed	I
	salt and pepper	
I	small basketcherry tomatoes, stems removed	I
I	orange for garnish	I

Cut little slits in the lamb and insert the slivers of garlic. Combine the olive oil and mint and brush on the surface of the lamb. Grill over moderately high heat until well-browned on the outside, but still a little pink on the inside. Let the lamb rest about 15 minutes. Wash and prepare the watercress, breaking the stems into bite-size pieces and trying to keep the leaves intact. Combine the olive oil, vinegar, mustard, garlic, salt and pepper and mix well. Toss the watercress and cherry tomatoes with the vinaigrette. Distribute the salad on four plates. Slice the lamb into fairly thin slices and arrange them on top of the salad. Cut an orange into thin slices. Cut each slice from one side through to the centre and then pull each side of the cut in opposite directions, producing a curl. Place an orange curl on top of each serving of lamb. Serves 8 or more.

Seafood Salad with White Wine Vinaigrette

2	red or yellow peppers	2
I dozen	extra large shrimp, shelled and deveined	I dozen
18	mussels (washed under running water to remove sand)	18
18	clams	18
I dozen	very large sea scallops	I dozen
	olive oil for grilling	
I	avocado, peeled and diced	I
I	bunch of watercress, torn into pieces	I
	vinaigrette made with white wine (recipe follows)	

Grill the whole peppers on the barbecue quickly over high heat until blackened all over. Place them in a paper bag for 5 or 10 minutes to sweat. Remove them and peel the blackened skin off. Cut the peppers into bite-size pieces and reserve. Peel the shrimp, leaving the tail intact. Brush them with olive oil and grill them over hot coals until they turn pink. Remove them to a serving bowl. Place the mussels on the grill. Barbecue until they open wide and remove to the serving bowl. Discard any mussels that do not open. Place the clams on the grill and cook until the shells open. Remove them to the serving bowl. Discard any that do not open. Brush the scallops with olive oil and grill over very hot coals until brown on the outside and just opaque or cooked through on the inside. Let cool to room temperature or refrigerate until chilled and add the peppers, avocado and watercress. Add the vinaigrette and toss gently until the salad is well-combined. Carefully spoon the salad into the clear glass serving bowl. Serve with crusty loaves of bread and garnish with lemon wedges. Serves 6.

White Wine Vinaigrette

1 cup	olive oil	250 mL
1/4 cup	white wine vinegar	50 mL
2 tbsp	lemon juice	25 mL
1	clove garlic crushed	1
2 tsp	Dijon mustard	10 mL

Combine all ingredients and stir or shake well.

Chicken and Almond Salad with Thyme Croutons

6	boneless chicken breast halves, skin on	6
2	cloves garlic, sliced	2
	olive oil for grilling	
6	slices of crusty bread	6
2 tbsp	fresh thyme, chopped	25 mL
1/4 cup	olive oil	50 mL
1/2 cup	olive oil	125 mL
2 tbsp	white wine vinegar	25 mL
1/2 tsp	Dijon mustard	2 mL
	salt and freshly ground pepper	
1	head butter lettuce, torn into pieces	1
1	avocado, peeled and sliced	1
3/4 cup	almonds, sliced	175 mL

Lift the skin on the chicken breasts and shove some garlic slices underneath. Brush the chicken with olive oil and grill, turning once, until golden on the outside and just cooked through on the inside. Combine the 1/4 cup olive oil with the fresh thyme and brush the slices of bread with it. Grill alongside the chicken until croutons are lightly toasted on both sides. Reserve for garnish. Combine the 1/2 cup olive oil, wine vinegar, mustard, salt and pepper and mix well. Toast the almond slices on an ungreased baking sheet in a 400°F oven until golden brown. Place the lettuce in a bowl and toss with the vinaigrette. Divide lettuce on 6 plates. Arrange a few slices of avocado over the lettuce. Slice the chicken breasts into 1/2 inch thick slices and arrange on top. Scatter almonds over the chicken and avocado. Garnish with a crouton. Serves 6.

Grilled Salad Niçoise

2 lbs	fresh tuna steak, cut about 1 inch thick	1 kg
	freshly ground black pepper	
	olive oil for grilling	
16-20	large slices of potato, cut 1/2 inch thick	16-20
3/4 lb	fresh green beans, stems removed	375 g
3/4 lb	fresh yellow beans, stems removed	375 g
1 cup	olive oil	250 mL
1/3 cup	white wine vinegar	75 mL
2 tbsp	lemon juice	25 mL
1	clove garlic, crushed	1
1 tsp	Dijon mustard	5 mL
	salt and freshly ground pepper	
1	head of red lettuce	1
1	head of Boston lettuce	1
1	head of leaf lettuce	1
	fresh basil leaves	
1/2 pint	red cherry tomatoes	
1/2 pint	yellow cherry tomatoes	
1 cup	black olives	250 mL
8	large eggs, hard-boiled, peeled and halved	8
2	cans flat anchovy fillets, drained	2
1/2 cup	capers, drained	125 mL

Sprinkle the tuna on both sides with pepper. Grill over hot coals, brushing with olive oil and turning once, until the tuna is browned on the outside and just cooked through. Brush the potato slices with olive oil and grill over moderately hot coals until browned on the outside and tender when pricked with a fork. Drop the beans into boiling water and cook for about one minute. Drain and refresh with cold running water and then pat dry. Combine the 1 cup of olive oil, lemon juice, wine vinegar, garlic, mustard, salt and pepper. Arrange one leaf of each type of lettuce on each of 8 plates. Add a few basil leaves, a few yellow and red cherry tomatoes, a few olives, 2 egg halves, capers, anchovies, green and yellow beans, potatoes and a few thin slices of grilled tuna. Pass the vinaigrette separately. Serves 8.

Seared Sea Scallop Salad
with Orange Vinaigrette

16-20	large sea scallops	16-20
2	large red onions, peeled and cut into eighths	2
	olive oil for grilling	
	freshly ground white pepper	
1	head Boston lettuce	1
1	head red lettuce	1
4	little bunches of mâche lettuce	4
8	chive stems	8
	orange vinaigrette (recipe follows)	

Brush the scallops with a mixture of the olive oil and a little white pepper. Grill over very hot coals, brushing with the oil and turning once, about 1 or 2 minutes a side, until the outside is seared and the inside is just cooked. Brush the red onion with the oil and pepper mixture and grill over hot coals until browned on the outside but still a little crunchy on the inside. Wash, dry and tear the Boston and red lettuce leaves into bite-size pieces. Arrange the lettuce on 4 individual plates. Place the scallops on top of the lettuce. Scatter the onion wedges around the scallops. Place the mâche lettuce in the centre. Set a pair of chive stems across the mâche. Drizzle the vinaigrette over top of the salad and serve. Serves 4.

Orange Vinaigrette

1/3 cup	olive oil	75 mL
1/4 cup	orange juice	50 mL
1 tbsp	orange zest	15 mL
1 tbsp	fresh sage, minced	15 mL
	salt and freshly ground pepper	

Combine the olive oil, orange juice and zest, sage, salt and pepper and mix well.

Curried Chicken Salad

6	boneless, skinless chicken breast halves	6
2 tsp	curry powder	10 mL
	olive oil for grilling	
1	head of leaf lettuce or Boston lettuce	1
1 cup	purple or black seedless grapes	250 mL
2/3 cup	pecan halves	150 mL
1/2 cup	mayonnaise	125 mL
2 tbsp	curry powder	25 mL
1-2 tsp	milk	5-10 mL
1	navel orange	1

Rub the chicken breasts with the curry powder, brush with olive oil and grill over hot coals, brushing with the oil and turning once, until the chicken is browned a little on the outside and no longer pink on the inside. Cut the chicken into bite-size pieces. In a bowl, combine the chicken, grapes, pecans, mayonnaise and curry powder, and mix well. Add the milk to dilute the mayonnaise a little. Arrange several lettuce leaves on 4 salad plates. Heap several spoonfuls of salad onto the lettuce. Cut the stem-end off the orange and then cut 4 slices of orange. Cut each orange slice to the centre, pull the two sides apart and set the orange on top of the salad. Squeeze a little juice from the ends of the orange over the 4 plates. Serves 4.

Suzanna's Shrimp Salad

16	giant shrimp, raw with the shells on	16
	olive oil or olive oil with garlic essence for grilling	
1	head ruby lettuce	1
1	head Boston lettuce	1
1	head endive	1
1	avocado, peeled pitted and cut into 8 wedges	1
1/2 cup	olive oil	125 mL
2 tbsp	lemon juice	25 mL
1/4 cup	white wine vinegar	50 mL
1 tbsp	fresh dill, chopped	15 mL
2	cloves garlic, crushed	2

Brush the shrimp with olive oil and grill over hot coals until they turn pink and are opaque throughout. Arrange torn lettuce leaves on four salad plates. Combine the olive oil, lemon juice, white wine vinegar, dill and garlic, and mix well. Set two wedges of avocado on top of the lettuce on each plate. Peel the shells from the shrimp, leaving the tails intact. Arrange the shrimp on top of the lettuce. Pour the vinaigrette over the salad. Serves 4 as a luncheon salad. This recipe can be transformed into a starter by serving 2 of these giant shrimp on a whole lettuce leaf with a wedge of avocado and

Mushroom and Black Olive Salad

I lb	assorted fresh mushrooms—crimini, shitaki, chanterelles, portabello or morels	500 g
1/4 cup	olive oil	50 mL
2 tbsp	fresh rosemary leaves, finely chopped	25 mL
1/3 cup	olive oil	75 mL
2 tbsp	balsamic vinegar	25 mL
I tsp	Dijon mustard	5 mL
I	clove garlic, crushed	I
	salt and freshly ground pepper	
1/2	head radicchio	1/2
I	head Boston lettuce	I
1/2	head chicory	1/2
1/2 cup	black olives	125 mL

Clean and trim the mushrooms. Combine the 1/4 cup olive oil and rosemary. Brush the mushrooms with the mixture and grill over moderately hot coals, brushing with the oil and turning frequently, until the mushrooms are a little crisp around the edges yet tender. Cool. If the mushrooms are large, slice them into manageable pieces. Combine the olive oil, balsamic vinegar, Dijon mustard, garlic, salt and pepper and mix well. Wash and dry the lettuce. Tear into large pieces and place in a bowl. Add the vinaigrette and toss well. Place the lettuce leaves on four salad plates. Scatter a few olives on each plate and a portion of the grilled mushrooms. Serves 4.

Joanne and Stan's Grilled Salad

I	large eggplant	I
2	large purple onions	2
2	large firm red tomatoes	2
	salt to taste	
3/4 cup	extra virgin olive oil	175 mL
I/2 cup	fresh basil, chopped fine	125 mL

Trim the ends from the eggplant and cut into I/2 inch thick slices. Sprinkle the slices lightly with salt and allow to drain on paper towels for 30 minutes. Rinse lightly and pat dry with paper towel. Slice the purple onions and tomatoes into I/2 inch thick slices. Brush the onions and tomatoes with olive oil and sprinkle with salt. Skewer the onions with very thin wooden skewers, that have been soaked in water for an hour, until the sharp end comes through the sides, leaving the dull end longer for easier handling. This prevents onions from falling apart. Brush the eggplant slices lightly with some of the olive oil. Grill the slices over medium-hot coals until browned and tender when pierced with a fork, approximately 4 minutes per side. Grill the tomatoes and onions in the same fashion, turning them over with a metal spatula to avoid breakage. Remove skewers from onions. Arrange in a pattern (eggplant, onion, tomato) in a serving dish and sprinkle with fresh basil when cool. Serve at room temperature.

Chicken and Tomato Salad

6	boneless, skinless chicken breast halves	6
	olive oil for grilling	
1/2 cup	whole toasted hazelnuts, skins removed	125 mL
3	tomatoes, chopped into 1 inch pieces	3
1	avocado peeled, pitted and chopped into 1 inch pieces	1
1 tbsp	fresh basil, minced	15 mL
	vinaigrette (recipe follows)	

Brush the chicken breasts with olive oil and grill over hot coals about four minutes a side until they are browned on the outside and just cooked through inside. Cool the breasts at room temperature and chop into 1 inch cubes. Place chicken in a salad bowl. Add hazelnuts, tomatoes, avocado and basil. Pour vinaigrette over salad and toss well. Serves 4-6.

Vinaigrette

1/2 cup	olive oil	125 mL
1/4 cup	white wine vinegar	50 mL
1/2 tsp	Dijon mustard	2 mL
1 tbsp	lemon juice	15 mL

Combine olive oil, vinegar, mustard and lemon juice and mix well.

POULTRY

Pineapple Chicken

1/2 cup	pineapple juice	125 mL
1/4 cup	brown sugar	50 mL
1 tsp	fresh ginger, grated	5 mL
1/4 cup	soya sauce	50 mL
2	garlic cloves, peeled and crushed	2
2 tbsp	olive oil	25 mL
12	boneless chicken breast halves	12
1	whole fresh pineapple	1

Combine the first six ingredients in a dish and add the chicken breasts. Marinate for about one hour at room temperature or overnight in the refrigerator. Trim the foliage and outer skin from the pineapple and cut it into eight long wedges, removing the hard inner core from each wedge. Remove the chicken breasts from the marinade and grill over hot coals, along with the wedges of pineapple. Brush both with the marinade. Turn the chicken once and grill until nicely browned on the outside and no longer pink on the inside. Turn the pineapple wedges frequently and grill until glazed brown. Serves 6.

Chicken Fajitas

1/2 cup	olive oil	125 mL
1 tbsp	red wine vinegar	15 mL
1/4 cup	soya sauce	50 mL
2 tsp	Worcestershire sauce	10 mL
3 tsp	garlic, peeled and crushed	15 mL
2 tsp	Tabasco sauce	10 mL
1 1/2 tsp	dry mustard	7 mL
1 tsp	freshly ground black pepper	5 mL
8	boneless chicken breast halves	8
1	red pepper, seeded and sliced into wide strips	1
1	green pepper, seeded and sliced into wide strips	1
2	medium onions, peeled and sliced thickly	2
2 tbsp	olive oil	25 mL
	guacamole (recipe follows)	
	tomato salsa (recipe follows)	
	sour cream	
8	fresh soft tortillas	8

Combine the first eight ingredients and add the chicken breasts. Marinate for 1 hour at room temperature or overnight in the refrigerator. Brown the peppers and onions in the 2 tbsp olive oil until softened and slightly brown. Barbecue the chicken over hot coals, brushing with the marinade and turning once, until the inside is no longer pink and the outside is nicely browned. Remove to a platter and slice the chicken breasts thinly. Serve the chicken slices with bowls of guacamole, salsa, sour cream and the peppers and onions. Pile the ingredients onto warmed soft tortillas and roll up to eat. Serves 4.

Guacamole

1	ripe avocado	1
2 tsp	lime juice	10 mL
1 tbsp	fresh cilantro, finely chopped	15 mL
1 tbsp	onion, finely chopped	15 mL
1	tomato, seeded and finely chopped	1
	hot pepper sauce to taste	
1/4 tsp	salt	2 mL

Cut the avocado in half and remove the pit. Scoop out the flesh. Mash the avocado and add the lime juice, cilantro, onion, tomato, hot pepper sauce and salt. Mix well and cover. Chill in the refrigerator if not ready to use immediately. Makes just under one cup.

Salsa

5	tomatoes	5
1/4 cup	green onions, chopped	50 mL
1/3 cup	fresh cilantro, chopped	75 mL
1/2	jalapeño pepper, seeded and minced	1/2
1 tbsp	olive oil	15 mL
1 tbsp	lime juice	15 mL
2	cloves garlic, minced	2
	salt and pepper	

Combine all ingredients and let sit for a half hour at room temperature. Cover and refrigerate if not ready to use. Try not to make more than 2 hours ahead of time.

Sage Chicken with Fresh Pear Chutney

1/2 cup	olive oil	125 mL
2 tbsp	fresh sage, finely chopped	25 mL
2 tbsp	lemon juice	25 mL
12	boneless, skinless chicken breast halves	12
	fresh pear chutney (recipe follows)	

Marinate the chicken breasts in the olive oil, sage and lemon juice for an hour at room temperature or overnight in the refrigerator. Grill the chicken breasts over hot coals until the inside is no longer pink and the outside is nicely browned. Serve with the fresh chutney. Serves 6.

Fresh Pear Chutney

4	pears, cored and finely chopped	4
1/3 cup	fresh mint, finely chopped	75 mL
1/4 cup	red pepper, finely chopped	50 mL
1/2	jalapeño pepper, seeded and minced	1/2
3 tsp	fresh ginger, seeded and minced	15 mL
1	garlic clove, crushed	1
1/4 cup	wine vinegar	50 mL
2 tbsp	honey	25 mL

Combine the honey and wine vinegar and blend well. Add the remaining ingredients to the honey and vinegar mixture and let the chutney sit for an hour.

Marmalade Curry Chicken

1/3 cup	marmalade	75 mL
2 tbsp	olive oil	25 mL
2 tbsp	white wine vinegar	25 mL
I	clove garlic, peeled and crushed	I
I tbsp	curry powder	15 mL
12	boneless, skinless chicken breast halves	12
I	navel orange cut into 6 wedges (for garnish)	I

Combine the marinade ingredients and add the chicken breasts. Marinate for an hour at room temperature or longer in the refrigerator. Grill the chicken over moderately hot coals, brushing with the marinade and turning once or twice as necessary, until the outside is nicely glazed and the inside is no longer pink. Serve with wedges of fresh orange. Serves 6.

Red Currant Glazed Chicken Legs

3 tbsp	olive oil	45 mL
1/3 cup	red currant jelly	75 mL
1 tbsp	honey	15 mL
2 tbsp	Dijon mustard	25 mL
3	garlic cloves, crushed	3
8	chicken legs split into thighs and drumsticks	8

Combine glaze ingredients and heat for about 4 minutes over moderate heat. Brush the glaze on the pieces of chicken and grill over moderately hot coals, brushing with the marinade and turning until the chicken is no longer pink inside and is nicely glazed on the outside. Serves 8.

Skewered Chicken with Baby Vegetables

1/3 cup	white or red wine vinegar	75 mL
1/2 cup	olive oil	125 mL
2 tbsp	fresh rosemary, finely chopped	25 mL
2	cloves garlic, crushed	2
1 1/2 lbs	skinless, boneless chicken breasts	750 g
12	baby zucchini	12
12	baby pattypan squashes	12
12	baby mushrooms	12

Combine the vinegar, oil, rosemary and garlic and add the chicken breasts. Marinate for one hour at room temperature or several hours in the refrigerator. Cut the chicken into chunks and place alternately on the skewers with the vegetables. Place over moderately hot coals and barbecue on all sides, brushing frequently with the marinade, until done. Serves 6.

Green Chicken

1/2 cup	extra virgin olive oil	125 mL
2 tsp	green peppercorns, crushed	10 mL
1 tbsp	fresh parsley, chopped	15 mL
1 tbsp	fresh thyme leaves, stripped from their stems	15 mL
1 tbsp	fresh basil, finely cut	15 mL
12	boneless, skinless chicken breast halves	12

Combine all ingredients but the chicken, and stir to combine. Add the chicken breasts and marinate an hour at room temperature or longer in the refrigerator. Grill over hot coals, brushing with the marinade and turning once, cooking for a few minutes on each side until the outsides are browned and the inside is no longer pink. Serves 6.

Jerk Chicken

I	medium onion, peeled and quartered	I
I	clove garlic, peeled and halved	I
	a portion of a Habañero pepper, seeded and halved or 2 serrano or jalapeño peppers, seeded and halved	
2 tbsp	soya sauce	25 mL
1/4 cup	red wine vinegar	50 mL
2 tbsp	vegetable oil	25 mL
I tbsp	brown sugar	15 mL
I tsp	allspice	5 mL
1/4 tsp	nutmeg	I mL
1/2 tsp	cinnamon	2 mL
1/2 tsp	black pepper	2 mL
1/2 tsp	salt	2 mL
8	skinless, boneless chicken breast halves	8

Chop the onion, garlic and chili peppers in a food processor until they are finely chopped. Add the soya sauce, vinegar, oil, brown sugar, spices and seasonings and process until well combined. Cut or tear chicken breasts in half, lengthwise. Marinate the chicken breasts for one hour at room temperature, or longer in the refrigerator. Grill over hot coals, brushing with the marinade and turning once, until the chicken is no longer pink inside. Serves 4.

Barbecued Chickenburgers

2 lbs	ground chicken	I kg
I tbsp	fresh thyme	15 mL
I cup	barbecue sauce	250 mL
6	hamburger buns	6
I	large Spanish onion, peeled and thickly sliced	I
	olive oil for grilling	
2	tomatoes, sliced	2
2	large dill pickles, sliced	2

Mix the thyme into the ground chicken and form into 6 oversize burgers, about 1/2 inch thick. Brush with barbecue sauce and grill over very hot coals, brushing with the sauce and turning once, until the burgers are cooked through and the outside is well-browned. In the meantime, brush the onions with olive oil and grill alongside the burgers. Serve the chickenburgers with the onions, tomatoes and pickles. Serves 6.

Chickenburgers with Apple Onion Chutney

2 lbs	ground chicken	1 kg
1	onion, chopped	1
1 tbsp	fresh sage, finely chopped	15 mL
6	hamburger buns	6
	apple onion chutney (recipe follows)	

Add the chopped onion and 1 tbsp fresh sage into the ground chicken. Form into 6 generous-size patties, about 1/2 inch thick. Refrigerate until ready to use. Grill the burgers over hot coals until cooked through and well-browned on the outside. Put the burgers in the burger buns and top with a few spoonfuls of chutney. Serves 6.

Apple Onion Chutney

5	large cooking apples, cored and chopped	5
I	onion, peeled and chopped	I
3	garlic cloves, peeled and finely chopped	3
1/3 cup	brown sugar	75 mL
1/3 cup	wine vinegar	75 mL
I cup	apple cider	250 mL
1/3 cup	raisins	75 mL
1/3 cup	golden raisins	75 mL
1/2 cup	dried cherries	125 mL
1/2 cup	dates, chopped	125 mL
1/3 cup	dried currants	75 mL
1/3 cup	fresh sage, chopped	75 mL

Combine all the chutney ingredients, except the sage, in a large saucepan and bring to a boil over medium heat. Reduce the heat to low and simmer about an hour until the chutney thickens. Stir in the fresh sage and simmer a few minutes more. Cool to room temperature and serve. It will keep refrigerated in a large sterile jar with a tight-fitting lid for several months.

Mango Chicken

16	boneless, skinless chicken breast halves	16
2	mangos	2
1/4 cup	fresh lime juice	250 mL
	zest from one lime	
3 tbsp	vegetable oil	45 mL
1/4 tsp	salt	1 mL
1/4 tsp	white pepper	1 mL

Peel the outer skin from the mango, cut the flesh into large chunks and place in the bowl of a food processor. Add the lime juice and zest, oil and seasoning. Process until blended. Place the chicken in a dish and cover with half of the marinade. Let sit at room temperature for an hour, or in the refrigerator overnight. Grill the chicken breasts over moderately hot coals until they are cooked through. Serve the chicken with the remaining sauce on the side. Serves 8.

Paprika Chicken with Nasturtium Butter

1/2 cup	olive oil	125 mL
2 tbsp	paprika	25 mL
1/2 tbsp	Dijon mustard	
	salt and freshly ground black pepper	
12	boneless, skinless chicken breast halves	12
	nasturtium butter (recipe follows)	

Mix the olive oil with the paprika, mustard, salt and pepper. Brush on the chicken breasts and grill over hot coals until the chicken is cooked through. Serve chicken with a dish of nasturtium butter. Serves 6.

Nasturtium Butter

1/4 cup	butter, softened	50 mL
1 tbsp	minced green onion	15 mL
1/3 cup	nasturtium blossoms and leaves, finely cut and firmly packed	75 mL
	few drops of hot pepper sauce	

Cream the butter in a small bowl. Add the onion, nasturtium blossoms and leaves, and the hot pepper sauce. Combine well. Place the butter mixture on a sheet of waxed paper and shape into a log about 1 1/4 inches thick. Roll tightly in the waxed paper and twist the ends. Chill one half hour, until firm. Unroll the nasturtium butter and slice into disks about a half inch thick.

Grilled Club Sandwiches

1/4 cup	olive oil	50 mL
2 tbsp	lemon juice	25 mL
1/2 tsp	dried thyme	2 mL
	salt and freshly ground pepper	
4	boneless, skinless chicken or turkey breast halves	4
1 or 2	tomatoes, sliced	1 or 2
4	leaves of fresh, leaf lettuce	4
12	strips of bacon, fried	12
	mayonnaise	
	butter	
1	loaf homemade white or whole wheat bread	1
4	large dill pickles	1

Combine the olive oil, lemon juice and thyme. Brush the chicken breasts with this mixture and grill over hot coals until browned on the outside and cooked through in the centre. Cool the chicken. Cut 12 slices of bread about half an inch thick. For toasted sandwiches, you can grill the bread over moderately hot coals until it is nicely browned on both sides or just toast the bread in a toaster. Place 4 slices of bread on a work surface and spread with mayonnaise. Slice the chicken breasts lengthwise into half inch slices and place on the 4 slices of bread. Cover chicken with lettuce leaves and sprinkle with salt and freshly ground pepper. Place 4 slices of bread on top of the chicken and lettuce and spread with mayonnaise again. Add the tomatoes and bacon, and finish off with a buttered slice of bread. Cut on the diagonal and serve with a dill pickle. Serves 4.

Mr Walla's
Barbecued Chicken

8	pieces of chicken, including thighs, drumsticks and breasts	8
	butter or olive oil	
	lemon juice	
	paprika	
	salt and pepper	
	mesquite or hickory wood chips	

Melt the butter and add the lemon juice, paprika, salt and pepper. Set the barbecue at its lowest setting. Place mesquite or hickory chips (that have been soaked in water about fifteen minutes) on the coals. Brush the chicken pieces with the butter mixture and place on the grill. Barbecue with the lid of the grill down. Baste and turn the chicken about every half hour for about 2 hours. In Joe's words, "Cook it on the smoke, not the fire." Barbecue until the chicken is cooked through. Test by piercing with a skewer. If the juice runs clear, it is done. Don't rush it; it will be worth the wait. Serve it with a good old-fashioned coleslaw. Serves 4.

Garlic Cumin Chicken

6	garlic cloves, unpeeled	6
I tbsp	fresh oregano, chopped	15 mL
I tsp	cumin, ground	5 mL
1/4 cup	lime juice	50 mL
I tbsp	olive oil	15 mL
	salt and freshly ground pepper	
12	boneless, skinless chicken breast halves	12

Toast the garlic cloves in a 375°F oven until soft inside; about 15 minutes. Peel the cloves and mash into a paste. Add the other ingredients and combine well. Spread the paste over the chicken and marinate for one hour at room temperature or up to 24 hours in the refrigerator. Grill the chicken over moderately hot coals, turning once, until the chicken is cooked through. Serves 6.

Peaches and Chicken

8	chicken thighs	8
I	peach, peeled, pitted and mashed	I
2 tbsp	olive oil	25 mL
I tbsp	honey	15 mL
I tbsp	balsamic vinegar	15 mL
I	garlic clove, crushed	I
	salt and pepper	
2	peaches	2
	olive oil for grilling the peaches	

Combine the peach, olive oil, honey, balsamic vinegar, garlic salt and pepper and add the chicken. Marinate for 4 hours in the refrigerator. Peel the 2 peaches, cut them in half, then in half again and discard the pits. Grill the chicken thighs over moderately hot coals, brushing with the marinade and turning to prevent over-browning, until the chicken is cooked through. Start grilling the peaches half way through cooking the chicken thighs. Brush the peaches with the olive oil and turn once. Grill until the peaches are cooked through and glazed a little on the outside. Serve the chicken with the peaches. Serves 4.

Maple Glazed
Chicken Breasts

8	boneless, skinless chicken breast halves	8
2 tbsp	olive oil	25 mL
I tbsp	green onion, minced	15 mL
4 tbsp	pure maple syrup	60 mL
2 tbsp	Dijon mustard	25 mL

Heat the oil in a small saucepan over moderate heat and add the green onions. Sauté until lightly browned. Add the maple syrup and mustard and bring to the boil. Simmer a few minutes until thickened. Brush the chicken with the maple mixture and grill over moderately hot coals, brushing with the sauce and turning once, until the chicken is nicely glazed on the outside and cooked through. Heat the leftover sauce on the edge of the grill until it comes to a boil. Serve it with the chicken. Serves 4.

Honey Curry Chicken

8	chicken thighs	8
3 tbsp	honey	45 mL
1/4 cup	curry powder	50 mL
1/3 cup	olive oil	75 mL

Trim any excess fat and extra skin from the chicken thighs. Combine the honey, curry powder and oil in a dish and add the chicken thighs. Marinate for 1 hour at room temperature or longer in the refrigerator covered. Grill over moderate coals slowly, brushing with the oil mixture, and turning as needed to prevent over-browning of the chicken. Serves 4.

Hazelnut Chicken

1/2 cup	hazelnut butter (recipe follows)	125 mL
6 tbsp	peanut oil	90 mL
1 tbsp	Dijon mustard	15 mL
12	boneless, skinless chicken breast halves	12

Combine the first three ingredients and mix well. Cut the chicken breast halves in half so that there are 24 pieces of chicken. Put the chicken breasts in the marinade and let the ingredients marinate for one hour at room temperature or up to 24 hours in the refrigerator. Grill the chicken over hot coals, brushing with the marinade and turning to prevent over-browning, until the chicken is no longer pink inside. Serves 6.

Hazelnut Butter

Place 3 cups of hazelnuts on a cookie sheet in a 400°F oven for 5 to 8 minutes, until the hazelnuts are toasted a little. Cool a few minutes and then rub them between your hands to remove some of the skins. Put the nuts in a food processor and grind until fairly smooth and spreadable.

Chili Pepper Chicken

1	jalapeño pepper	1
1	small hot red chili pepper	1
1	large red pepper	1
3	cloves garlic, peeled	3
1	shallot, peeled	1
2 - 3 tbsp	olive oil	25 - 45 mL
	salt and freshly ground pepper	
8	boneless, chicken breast halves, skin on	8

Grill the peppers over hot coals until blackened. Place in a paper bag to sweat for 10 minutes. Peel the blackened skin from the peppers. Remove the inner membranes and seeds from the peppers. Chop the garlic and shallot in the bowl of a food processor until minced. Add the peppers, olive oil, salt and pepper, and process until the mixture is a smooth paste. Rub the chili mixture on the chicken breasts and grill over moderately hot coals until the chicken is no longer pink on the inside. Serves 8.

Kids' Chicken Wings

3 or 4	dozen chicken wings	3 or 4
1/2	bottle President's Choice Gourmet Barbecue Sauce	1/2
	half lemon	
	vegetable oil for grilling	

Cut the tips from each chicken wing and discard, or save for another use. Cut through the remaining joint, giving you two pieces of chicken for each wing. Place the wings in a bowl and sprinkle them with the oil. Place them over moderately hot coals and grill, brushing with the oil and turning them once until they are golden brown on the outside. Remove the wings to a platter and coat them with the barbecue sauce. Put them back on the grill, and turn and baste until the meat is pulled easily from the bones, and the sauce has turned into a delicious glaze on the surface of the wings. Load them on a platter and drizzle the juice from the lemon over the wings. Serves 6.

MEAT

Ginger Bay Leaf Steak

3 lbs	boneless steak, cut into cubes	1 1/2 kg
1 cup	soya sauce	250 mL
1/2 cup	sherry	125 mL
1/4 cup	brown sugar	50 mL
2 tbsp	fresh ginger, grated	25 mL
2	cloves garlic, crushed	2
	bay leaves	

Combine all the ingredients, except the bay leaves and marinate for an hour at room temperature, or 24 hours in the refrigerator. Place the chunks of beef on skewers with the bay leaves. Grill over hot coals, turning frequently and brushing with the marinade, until the beef is cooked as desired. Serves 6.

Steak with Wild Mushroom Salsa

3 lbs	sirloin steak cut into 6 steaks	1 1/2 kg
2 tsp	cracked black pepper	10 mL
	wild mushroom salsa (recipe follows)	

Sprinkle the steaks with the cracked pepper. Grill over very hot coals until browned on the outside and cooked as desired on the inside. Serve with the mushroom salsa on the side. Serves 6.

Wild Mushroom Salsa

1/3 cup	olive oil	75 mL
2 tbsp	balsamic vinegar	25 mL
3	garlic cloves crushed	3
1 tbsp	chopped fresh thyme	15 mL
8 oz	fresh crimini mushrooms	250 g
8 oz	fresh shitake mushrooms	250 g

Combine the oil, vinegar, garlic and thyme. Brush the mushrooms with the marinade and grill over moderate coals turning occasionally until the mushrooms are tender. Remove to a chopping block and coarsely chop the mushrooms. Add mushrooms to the marinade and stir to combine.

Peppered Steak with Hot Pepper Pesto

2 tbsp	black peppercorns	25 mL
8	filet mignon steaks	8
	hot pepper pesto (recipe follows)	

Put the peppercorns in a plastic bag. With a mallet or rolling pin, crush the peppercorns, leaving many large pieces. Sprinkle the pepper on the steaks and press into the surface of the beef with your fingers. Grill the steaks over very hot coals until the outside is well-browned and the inside is cooked as desired. Serve with the pesto. Serves 8.

Hot Pepper Pesto

2	red peppers	2
I	small hot red pepper	I
3/4 cup	fresh basil leaves	175 mL
1/4 cup	parmesan cheese	50 mL
I 1/2 tbsp	olive oil	20 mL
I 1/2 tbsp	balsamic vinegar	20 mL
3	garlic cloves, minced	

Grill the 3 peppers over very hot coals until the outer skin is blackened all over. Place the peppers in a paper bag to sweat for 10 minutes. Remove the peppers and peel away the outer skin. Do not wash the peppers as this will remove some of their oils and flavour. Remove the core, ribs and seeds. Chop the large peppers into big pieces and place in a food processor. Depending on your taste for hot food, place a portion or all of the hot pepper in the food processor as well. Add the basil leaves, cheese, olive oil, vinegar and garlic and process until well-blended, but still fairly granular. Refrigerate if not being used for a few hours. Return to room temperature before serving.

Honey Ginger Steak with Fresh Fruit Chutney

4	New York strip sirloin steaks	4
1/2 cup	soya sauce	125 mL
1/4 cup	honey	50 mL
1/4 cup	balsamic vinegar	50 mL
3 tbsp	fresh ginger, peeled and coarsely grated	45 mL
2	large garlic cloves, peeled and crushed	2
4	sprigs of fresh mint (for garnish)	4
	fresh fruit chutney (recipe follows)	

Combine the soya sauce, honey, balsamic vinegar, ginger and garlic in a dish and add the steaks. Let the steaks marinate for an hour at room temperature or up to 24 hours in the refrigerator. Grill the steaks over hot coals, brushing with the marinade and turning once, until cooked as desired. Serve with the fresh chutney. Garnish with mint. Serves 4.

Fresh Fruit Chutney

1/4 cup	wine vinegar	50 mL
2 tbsp	honey	25 mL
I	peach, peeled, pitted and chopped	I
4	plums, pitted and chopped	4
12	cherries, pitted and halved	12
1/3 cup	fresh mint, finely cut	75 mL
I	red pepper, seeded and chopped	I
1/2	jalapeño pepper, seeded, deveined and minced	1/2
I tbsp	fresh ginger, peeled and minced	15 mL
I	garlic clove, peeled and minced	I

Combine the wine vinegar, honey, fruit, mint, peppers, ginger and garlic. Let the chutney sit for at least half an hour. If made ahead, refrigerate up to 4 hours. The fruit is not at its best if made too far in advance.

Meat Loaf Burgers

2 tbsp	olive oil	
2	onions, finely chopped	2
1/2	green pepper, finely chopped	1/2
3	garlic cloves, minced	3
1 tbsp	fresh thyme, chopped	15 mL
1 tbsp	fresh rosemary, chopped	15 mL
2 lbs	ground beef	1 kg
1/2 lb	fresh pork sausage	250 g
1 tbsp	Dijon mustard	15 mL
2 tbsp	Worcestershire sauce	25 mL
1/2 tsp	Tabasco sauce	2 mL
1/3 cup	ketchup	75 mL
	salt and freshly ground pepper	
1/2 cup	barbecue sauce	125 mL

In a medium skillet, fry the onions, pepper and garlic lightly in the olive oil. Combine the remaining ingredients, except the barbecue sauce, and add the onion mixture. Form the mixture into 8 hamburger patties. Brush with the barbecue sauce and grill over moderately hot coals until done to perfection. Serves 8.

Red Wine Steak with Red Onion and Raisin Jam

3 tbsp	red wine	45 mL
2 tbsp	Worcestershire sauce	25 mL
1/2 cup	olive oil	125 mL
2 tsp	Dijon mustard	10 mL
4	cloves garlic, crushed	4
6	filet mignon steaks	6
	red onion and raisin jam (recipe follows)	

Combine the red wine, Worcestershire sauce, olive oil, mustard and garlic in a dish. Add the steaks and marinate about 4 hours or more in the refrigerator. Grill the steaks over moderately hot coals, brushing with the marinade and turning once, until cooked as desired. Serve with the jam. Serves 6.

Red Onion and Raisin Jam

2	large red onions, finely sliced	2
3 tbsp	brown sugar	45 mL
3/4 cup	red wine	175 mL
1/4 cup	balsamic vinegar	50 mL
1/2 cup	raisins	125 mL
	salt and freshly ground pepper	

Stir the onions and brown sugar together in a medium saucepan over moderate heat, until the mixture turns a golden brown and the juices thicken; about 20 minutes or more. Add the raisins, wine and vinegar and continue to stir until most of the liquid dries up. Season with salt and pepper. If not using within the hour, store covered in the refrigerator. Use within a few weeks. Heat a little before serving.

Mixed Grill

4	small beef tenderloins	4
4	lamb chops	4
1	pork tenderloin	1
1 lb	fresh sausage	500 g
	olive oil for grilling	
1	large sprig of fresh rosemary	1
	salt and pepper	

Heat a little olive oil in a small saucepan and add the rosemary. Cut the pork tenderloin into 4 equal portions. Brush all the meats with the oil and grill over very hot coals, brushing with the oil and sprinkling with salt and pepper, and turning once, until the meat is browned on the outside and cooked as desired on the inside. Divide the sausage into 4 equal portions. Serves 4.

Sesame Beef

1/2 cup	soya sauce	125 mL
2 tbsp	sesame oil	25 mL
2 tbsp	balsamic vinegar	25 mL
2 tsp	fresh ginger, peeled and grated	10 mL
3	cloves garlic, peeled and crushed	3
1 tbsp	brown sugar	15 mL
1/4 cup	sesame seeds, toasted	50 mL
1 1/2 lbs	sirloin steak, cut 1 1/2" thick	750 g

Combine the soya sauce, sesame oil, balsamic vinegar, ginger, garlic, brown sugar and sesame seeds. Add the steak and marinate overnight in the refrigerator. Grill the steak over hot coals, brushing with the marinade and turning once, until the steak is browned on the outside and grilled as desired on the inside. To serve, slice steak thinly. The marinade can be brought to a boil and reduced a little to pour over the steak. Serves 4.

Mike and Brenda's Beef Teriyaki

1 cup	soya sauce	250 mL
5 tbsp	sherry	75 mL
5 tbsp	demerara sugar	75 mL
2 tbsp	fresh ginger, grated	25 mL
2	cloves garlic, peeled and crushed	2
2 to 3 lbs	sirloin steak, cut into cubes	1 kg to 1 1/2 kg

Combine soya sauce, sherry, sugar, ginger and garlic and mix well. Add the steak and marinate from 2 to 6 hours in the refrigerator. Soak wooden skewers for an hour in water. Thread the chunks of beef onto the skewers. Grill over hot coals, brushing with the marinade and turning once, until the steak is cooked to desired degree. Serves 6.

Paul Conway's
Standing Rib Roast

I	standing rib roast with the bone in	I
2 or 3	garlic cloves, slivered	2 or 3
	La Grille Montreal Steak Spice by Club House or freshly ground black pepper	
	salt	

With a deboning knife, pierce through the round of beef in several places. Insert slivers of the garlic in the holes. Sprinkle the roast with the Montreal Steak Spice, or the black pepper, and place in the barbecue, prepared as mentioned above. Open the vents and close the cover. Grill the roast for an estimated 15 minutes per pound, checking the meat about 1/2 hour before finishing time. If you used the black pepper, sprinkle the roast with salt about 5 minutes before removing the roast from the barbecue. Wrap the roast in tin foil and let stand at room temperature for 10 minutes before carving. This allows the juices from the centre to expand to the outer edges of the beef.

Ginger Flank Steak

1 1/2 tsp	fresh ginger, grated	7 mL
4	garlic cloves, crushed	4
1 tbsp	fresh thyme leaves	15 mL
1/3 cup	soya sauce	75 mL
1 tbsp	vegetable oil	15 mL
1 1/2 lbs	flank steak	1 kg to 1 1/2 kg

Combine the ginger, garlic, thyme, soya sauce and vegetable oil. Mix well. Add the steak. Marinate up to 24 hours in the refrigerator. Grill about 5 minutes a side over hot coals, brushing with the marinade and turning once, until the steak is cooked as desired. Serves 6.

Honey Basil Pork

1/2 cup	honey	125 mL
2 tbsp	lemon juice	25 mL
1/4 cup	soya sauce	50 mL
4	garlic cloves, crushed	4
2 tbsp	fresh basil, finely cut	25 mL
2 tbsp	fresh parsley, chopped	25 mL
2	pork tenderloins, cut in half lengthwise	2

Combine everything but the pork in a small bowl and mix well. Add the pork and marinate 1 hour at room temperature or overnight in the refrigerator. Grill the tenderloins over hot coals, brushing with the marinade and turning, until they are brown on all sides and just barely pink on the inside. Serves 4.

Tropical Pork with Ricky's Rice and Peas

1/2 cup	soya sauce	125 mL
1/4 cup	white wine vinegar	50 mL
2 tbsp	lime juice	25 mL
	zest of 1 lime	
1 tsp	fresh ginger, peeled and grated	5 mL
1/4 cup	fresh mint, chopped	50 mL
1	large clove garlic, peeled and crushed	1
2	pork tenderloins	2
1	ugli fruit	1
1	starfruit	1
1	pineapple	1

Combine the first seven ingredients in a dish and add the pork. Marinate for one hour at room temperature or longer in the refrigerator. Cut the ugli fruit with the peel intact into sixteen pieces. Slice the starfruit into eight slices. Trim the outer skin and leaves from the pineapple and cut it into large chunks. Thread the fruit and pork onto eight skewers. Grill on the barbecue over hot coals, brushing with the marinade and turning, until the pork is no longer pink inside and is well browned on the outside. Serve with Ricky's Rice and Peas. Serves 4.

Ricky's Rice and Peas

1/2 cup	dried pinto beans	125 mL
1 cup	white rice	250 mL
3/4 cup	canned coconut milk	175 mL
1 1/4 cup	bean liquid	300 mL
	sprig of thyme	
1	chopped scallion	1
2 tsp	butter	10 mL
1 tsp	salt	5 mL

Soak the beans overnight in about 4 cups of water or bring the beans and water to a boil and then simmer until tender, about 1 or 2 hours. Drain the beans, reserving the liquid. Bring the coconut milk and bean liquid to a boil over high heat. Add the rice, thyme, scallion, butter and salt. Turn the heat to low and simmer 20 or 25 minutes until tender. Add the pinto beans and heat until the beans are as hot as the rice. Serves 4.

Citrus Pork

1/4 cup	lime juice	50 mL
1/2 cup	orange juice	125 mL
	zest of 1 lime	
	zest of 1 orange	
2 tbsp	balsamic vinegar	25 mL
1 tbsp	Dijon mustard	15 mL
3	garlic cloves, peeled and crushed	3
4	sprigs of fresh thyme chopped or 1 tsp (5 mL) of dried thyme	4
	salt and pepper	
1/4 cup	olive oil	50 mL
2	pork tenderloins cut in half, lengthwise wedges of lime (garnish)	2

Combine all the ingredients and let marinate for an hour or more. Brush the grill with some olive oil and grill over hot coals, turning as needed and brushing with the marinade, until the pork is barely pink in the centre. Garnish with lime wedges. Serves 4.

Old-fashioned Barbecue Spareribs

This recipe has been in the family for years. It was one of the first recipes for a dinner that I ever mastered and I wooed my future husband with it.

3-4 lbs	pork spareribs	1 1/2-2 kg
1/2 cup	onions, peeled and chopped	125 mL
2 tbsp	butter	25 mL
1 cup	water	250 mL
1/4 cup	vinegar	50 mL
2 1/2 tbsp	Worcestershire sauce	35 mL?
1/2 cup	lemon juice	125 mL
1/4 cup	brown sugar	50 mL
2 cups	bottled chili sauce	500 mL
1 tsp	salt	5 mL
3/4 tsp	paprika	3 mL

Cut the ribs into serving-size pieces. Place in a roasting pan, cover with foil and bake at 450°F for 15 minutes. Brown the onions in the melted butter. Add the remaining ingredients and simmer for 20 minutes. Brush the ribs with the barbecue sauce and place over moderately hot coals. Brush and turn frequently until the ribs are the way you like them. Serves 6.

Spiced Honey Pork
with Apples

1/4 cup	honey	50 mL
1/4 tsp	ginger	1 mL
1/4 tsp	cinnamon	1 mL
1/4 tsp	nutmeg	1 mL
1/4 tsp	curry powder	1 mL
1 tbsp	fresh oregano minced	15 mL
2	pork tenderloins	2
2	Granny Smith apples	2

Combine the honey with the spices and oregano and let stand for a half hour. Cut the pork into chunks and the apple into wedges, removing the core but leaving the skin on. Thread the pork and apples, alternately on 4 skewers. Place over hot coals and grill on all sides. For the last 2 minutes of grilling, brush with the spiced honey frequently. Serves 4.

Sausages with Apples and Sage

3 lbs	fresh sausage	1 1/2 kg
1/3 cup	olive oil	75 mL
2 tbsp	fresh sage, finely chopped	25 mL
4	Granny Smith apples, unpeeled and cut into halves	4
8	sprigs of fresh sage for garnish	8

Mix the sage into the olive oil. Brush the sausages and apples with the sage oil mixture and place on the grill. Grill over moderately hot coals, brushing and turning often, until the inside of the sausage is fully-cooked and the apples are golden brown on the outside and tender but still a little crunchy on the inside. If the apples are finished cooking before the sausages, remove them to a shelf on the inside of the barbecue away from the direct heat. Garnish with some fresh sage. Serves 8.

Pineapple Treacle Pork

2/3 cup	vegetable oil	150 mL
1/2 cup	pineapple juice	125 mL
1/4 cup	soya sauce	50 mL
1 tbsp	black treacle or molasses	15 mL
1 tsp	powdered ginger	5 mL
2	pork tenderloins	2
1	pineapple	1

Cut the tenderloins in half lengthwise. Combine the oil, juice, soya sauce, treacle and ginger in a baking dish and add the pork. Let marinate an hour at room temperature, or up to 24 hours in the refrigerator. Cut the outer skin from the pineapple and cut into 8 wedges, cutting away the hard inner core from each wedge. Remove the pork from the marinade and grill over hot coals, brushing with the marinade and turning once until the outside is well-browned and the inside is just a little pink. Brush the pineapple wedges and grill them alongside the pork, basting and turning, until browned on the outside and heated through. Serves 4.

Marmalade Pork

1/3 cup	marmalade	75 mL
1	garlic clove, peeled and crushed	1
1 tbsp	balsamic vinegar	15 mL
2 tbsp	olive oil	25 mL
	juice from one Clementine orange or small navel orange	
2	pork tenderloins	2

Combine all the ingredients, except the pork, in a dish. Grill the tenderloins over hot coals until the outside is browned. Reduce the heat, brush with the marinade and grill, brushing and turning, until the outside is glazed and the inside is just barely pink. Serves 4.

Skewered Ribs with Apples and Onions

The spareribs need to be cut in long strips for this recipe, so have the butcher prepare them for you at the supermarket. Choose the widest ribs you can find and ask the butcher to cut them in 2 inch widths across the bones. If lady apples or other varieties of small apples are hard to come by, substitute some cooking apples unpeeled and quartered.

3-4 lbs	pork spareribs	1 1/2-2 kg
12	small lady apples, unpeeled, halved and with stems intact and cores removed	12
6	cooking onions, peeled and cut in quarters	6
1 cup	barbecue sauce, preferably homemade	250 mL

Thread the sparerib strips, apples and onions on skewers, starting with the end of a rib. Add an apple, then wrap the rib around the apple and thread onto skewer. Add an onion and wrap the rib back the other way. Do not crowd the meat on the skewers as the pork may not cook through fast enough.

Continue in this fashion until you have 6 long skewers or 12 short ones. Brush the skewers with barbecue sauce and grill over moderately hot coals, turning and brushing with sauce, until the skewers are well-browned and cooked through. Serve over rice. Serves 6.

Orange Pork Medallions with Mangos

1/2 cup	olive oil	125 mL
2 tbsp	brown sugar	25 mL
3 tbsp	orange juice	45 mL
2 tsp	fresh rosemary, chopped	10 mL
2	garlic cloves, peeled and crushed	2
	salt and pepper	
2	pork tenderloins, cut crosswise into 1 inch slices	2
1	mango	1
1	orange, quartered	1

Combine the olive oil, brown sugar, orange juice, rosemary, garlic, salt and pepper. Place the pork in the oil mixture and let marinate an hour at room temperature or longer in the refrigerator. Cut the mango into long wedges, then cut the wedges into thirds. Thread the pork and mango chunks onto 4 skewers. Thread a chunk of orange on at the end. Grill the skewers over hot coals, basting and turning to prevent the mangos from burning, until the pork is cooked through. To serve, remove the pork and mangos from the skewer and squeeze the orange wedge over all. Serves 4.

Pork with Peanut Sauce

2	pork tenderloins, cut in half lengthwise	2
1/2 cup	vegetable oil	125 mL
1/4 cup	soya sauce	50 mL
2	cloves garlic, peeled and crushed	2
1 tbsp	fresh ginger, peeled and grated	15 mL
	peanut sauce (recipe to follow)	

Combine the vegetable oil, soya sauce, garlic and ginger. Mix well and add the tenderloins. Marinate one hour at room temperature or overnight in the refrigerator. Grill over hot coals until the outside is nicely browned and the inside is cooked through. Serve sliced with the peanut sauce. Serves 4.

Peanut Sauce

3 tbsp	peanut oil	45 mL
I or 2	cloves garlic, peeled and crushed	I or 2
I tbsp	onion, peeled and minced	15 mL
1/2 or I	whole jalapeño chili, seeded and minced	1/2 or I
1/2 cup	crunchy peanut butter	125 mL
1/2 tbsp	soya sauce	7 mL
1/2 tbsp	lemon juice	7 mL
I tbsp	demerara or brown sugar	15 mL
1/2 tsp	sambal oelek	2 mL

Heat the peanut oil in a small fry pan and add the garlic, onion and jalapeño chili. Fry just long enough to give the oil a little flavour and soften the vegetables. In a bowl, combine the peanut butter, soya sauce, sugar and chili sambal. Add the peanut oil mixture and combine well. Refrigerate until ready to use. Heat the peanut sauce before serving.

Butterflied Leg of Lamb with Mint and Garlic

The lamb in this recipe can be pounded with a mallet to make the thickness of the meat more uniform, but I seldom do this because grilling it, as is, provides a range of choices from well done to rare. If everyone likes their lamb medium rare, I get out the mallet.

1/2 cup	olive oil	125 mL
5	garlic cloves, peeled and crushed	5
1/4 cup	balsamic vinegar	50 mL
2 tbsp	fresh mint, chopped	25 mL
	salt & pepper	
1	boneless, butterflied leg of lamb	1

Combine marinade ingredients and add lamb. Marinate for an hour at room temperature or overnight in the refrigerator. Grill over moderately hot coals, brushing with the marinade and turning once, until the lamb is nicely browned on the outside and still a little pink on the inside. Serves 6 to 8, depending on the size of the leg.

Grilled Lamb
with Mint Pesto

1	boneless, butterflied leg of lamb	1
	olive oil	
4	garlic cloves, peeled	4
	salt & pepper	
	mint pesto (recipe follows)	

Flatten the thickest parts of the lamb by pounding it with a mallet. Cut 8 slits in the lamb. Cut the four garlic cloves in half lengthwise and place one in each of the slits. Brush the lamb with some olive oil and place over hot coals. Grill about ten minutes on each side, brushing with the olive oil. Sprinkle with salt and pepper near the end of cooking. Grill until the lamb is cooked as desired. Serve the lamb with the pesto. Serves 6 to 8 as a main course and 25 or more as an hors d'oeuvre.

Mint Pesto

1/3 cup	walnuts	75 mL
6	garlic cloves, peeled	6
2 cups	fresh mint leaves	500 mL
1/4 cup	olive oil	50 ml
1/4 cup	balsamic vinegar	50 mL

Combine the pesto ingredients in the bowl of a food processor fitted with a steel blade and process until the mixture is well combined but still course.

Skewered Lamb
with Peppers

1/2 cup	olive oil	125 mL
1/4 cup	balsamic vinegar	50 mL
1 tbsp	fresh rosemary, chopped	15 mL
2	garlic cloves, peeled and crushed	2
	salt and pepper	
1	leg of lamb	1
1	red pepper	1
1	yellow pepper	1
1	green pepper	1
32	red and yellow cherry tomatoes	32

Combine olive oil, vinegar, rosemary, garlic, salt and pepper in a dish. Cut the leg of lamb into chunks and add to the marinade. Marinate for 1 hour at room temperature or longer in the refrigerator. Cut the red and yellow peppers into chunks and thread onto the skewers with the lamb and the cherry tomatoes. Grill over hot coals, brushing with the marinade and turning to grill all sides. Serves 8.

Milliken Family Barbecued Lamb

I	leg of lamb	I
2	cloves garlic, peeled and slivered	2
	few sprigs of fresh rosemary	
	lemons	
	olive oil for grilling	

Prepare the lamb for the spit, by making little slits in the flesh of the lamb with the tip of a sharp knife. Insert the slivers of garlic and little pieces of rosemary in the slits. Run the spit through the leg of lamb as close to the centre as possible. If your spit is not equipped with prongs for securing the meat to the spit, you may want to fasten the meat further by lacing a string through the flesh in a few places, with a large needle and tying it onto the spit. Brush the lamb with olive oil, squeeze on lots of lemon juice and set the spit in place. Barbecue over moderate heat, brushing with oil and squeezing on lemon, until the roast is cooked as desired. The process should take a couple of hours. Serves 6 to 8 people, depending on the size of the leg of lamb.

The Sheepdog Handler's Barbecued Lamb

I	leg of lamb, deboned	I
	salt and pepper	
I	clove garlic, peeled and crushed	I
I tbsp	fresh thyme, chopped	15 mL
I tbsp	fresh basil, chopped	15 mL
3/4 cup	red wine	175 mL
1/2 cup	olive oil	125 mL
2 tbsp	lemon juice	25 mL
I	bay leaf	I
1/2 cup	butter	125 mL
	juice and rind of I lemon	
3 tbsp	fresh mint, chopped	45 mL

Combine all the ingredients in a dish and marinate the lamb for 24 hours, turning the meat about every 6 hours. Barbecue over moderate coals for about 45 minutes, brushing with the marinade and turning about every 6 to 7 minutes until grilled to desired degree of doneness. Melt the butter in a small saucepan on the edge of the grill. Add the juice and grated lemon rind, as well as the mint, and heat a few minutes. Serve with the lamb. Serves 6 to 8.

Mint Glazed Lamb Chops

1/3 cup	mint jelly	75 mL
1 tbsp	balsamic vinegar	15 mL
2 tbsp	olive oil	25 mL
1	clove garlic, peeled and crushed	1
	salt and freshly ground pepper	
8	lamb chops	8

Combine the marinade ingredients and mix well. Add the lamb chops and marinate for 1 hour at room temperature or overnight in the refrigerator. Grill over hot coals, brushing with the marinade and turning as needed to prevent over-browning, until the chops are barely pink inside. If desired, bring the remaining marinade to a boil over high heat and reduce, stirring occasionally, until thickened. Serve with the lamb chops. Serves 4.

Minted Lamb Chops

1/4 cup	bottled mint sauce	50 mL
1/4 cup	olive oil	50 mL
	salt and freshly ground pepper	
1/4 cup	fresh mint, chopped [optional]	50 mL
8	lamb chops	8

Combine the marinade ingredients and add the lamb chops. Marinate for an hour at room temperature or overnight in the refrigerator. Grill over hot coals, brushing with the marinade and turning once, until the chops are barely pink on the inside. Serves 4.

Paul Conway's Rabbit with Green Olives

1	whole rabbit	1
2/3 cup	olive oil	150 mL
1 tsp	dried rosemary	5 mL
1 1/2-2 tsp	dried thyme	7-10 mL
	black pepper	
2	cloves garlic, peeled and crushed	2
2 tbsp	Dijon mustard	25 mL
1/3 cup	lemon juice or flavoured vinegar	75 mL
16	large green olives	16
1	orange, cut into 4 wedges	1

Cut the head off the rabbit, if it is still attached, and reserve for stock. Combine the olive oil, rosemary, thyme, pepper, garlic, mustard and lemon juice or vinegar in a stainless steel bowl. Place the rabbit in a stainless steel bowl. Pour half of the marinade over the rabbit and let sit for an hour or less. Add the olives to the remaining bowl of marinade. Prepare the grill as described in Paul Conway's Standing Rib Roast recipe and set the rabbit on the barbecue, with the legs spread out on either side, over the place where there are no coals or where the volcanic plate covers the lava rocks. Grill for 30 minutes, brushing with the marinade. Add the olives to the grill over the coals or on the edge of the volcanic plates. Grill about another 15 minutes. The olives will be caramelized gold and the skin will break on the rabbit when it is done. It should be cooked to the bone, but not dry. Cut the rabbit into sections to serve and then reassemble them on a platter. Decorate the rabbit with the grilled olives and orange sections. Serves 4.

FISH

Citrus Salmon

When making the citrus zest for this recipe, use the large grater. The flavour is greatly enhanced by doing this.

4	salmon steaks	4
	juice of 1 lime	
	zest of 1 lime	
	juice of 1 orange	
	zest of 1 orange	
2	garlic cloves, peeled and crushed	2
1 tsp	fresh ginger, peeled and grated	5 mL
1/4 cup	olive oil	50 mL
1 tsp	honey	5 mL
1/2	jalapeño pepper, seeded and minced	1/2
4	wedges of lime	4

Combine juice and zest of the citrus fruit, garlic, ginger, olive oil, honey and jalapeño and add the salmon steaks. Marinate for one hour. Grill the steaks over hot coals, brushing frequently with the marinade, until the steaks are just turned opaque inside. Serve the steaks with wedges of lime. Serves 4.

Tuna With Black Bean Salsa

1 1/2 lbs	tuna steak, cut 1 inch thick	750 g
1 tbsp	olive oil	15 mL
1 tbsp	fresh lime juice	15 mL
	black bean salsa (recipe follows)	

Combine the remaining olive oil and lime juice and brush on the tuna. Place over hot coals and grill four to six minutes per side, until the outside is browned and the inside is just cooked. Serve with salsa. Serves 4.

Black Bean Salsa

I cup	dried black turtle beans washed and soaked in cold water overnight	250 mL
2	tomatoes, seeded and chopped	2
1/3 cup	fresh cilantro, chopped	75 mL
I	jalapeño pepper, seeded and minced	I
2 tbsp	fresh lime juice	25 mL
2 tbsp	olive oil	25 mL
I	avocado peeled, pitted and chopped	I

Drain the black beans and put in a saucepan with enough water to cover. Bring the beans to a boil and cook until they are tender, about I hour. Drain the beans, pass under cold running water, and combine with tomatoes, cilantro, jalapeño pepper, lime juice, olive oil and avocado. Allow the mixture to sit at room temperature about 1/2 hour before serving. If it is necessary to make it ahead, refrigerate up to 3 or 4 hours but do not add the avocado until ready to serve.

Swordfish Steak with Tropical Salsa

1 1/2 lbs	swordfish steak, cut 1 inch thick	750 mL
	olive oil for grilling	
	salt and pepper	
	tropical salsa (recipe follows)	

Cut the swordfish into 6 servings. Brush the swordfish steaks with a little olive oil and grill over hot coals, about 3 to 4 minutes a side, until the steaks are browned on the outside and just opaque on the inside. Serve with the salsa. Serves 6.

Tropical Salsa

1	ripe papaya, peeled, seeded and chopped	1
1	ripe mango, peeled, pitted and chopped	1
1/3 cup	fresh cilantro, chopped	75 mL
1/2 cup	green onions, chopped	125 mL
1/2	fresh jalapeño pepper, seeded and minced	1/2
2 tbsp	lemon juice	25 mL

Combine the six ingredients and let stand for half an hour at room temperature.

Salmon with
Lime Mint Butter

1/2 cup	lime juice	125 mL
1/2 cup	olive oil	125 mL
1/2 cup	fresh mint leaves, chopped	125 mL
6	salmon steaks	6
1/4 cup	fresh mint leaves, chopped	50 mL
1/4 cup	butter	50 mL
1 tsp	lime zest	5 mL
1 tsp	lime juice	5 mL
6	lime wedges	6

Combine lime juice, olive oil and 1/2 cup of mint. Add salmon steaks and marinate for an hour. Soften the butter with a fork and add remaining mint, lime zest and juice. Combine well. Form into a log shape, about an inch in diameter, on waxed paper, wrap tightly in the paper and refrigerate or freeze. Grill the steaks over hot coals, brushing frequently with the marinade and turning once, until the steaks are browned a little on the outside and just barely opaque throughout on the inside. Do not overcook. Unwrap the lime mint butter and slice into disks about half an inch thick. Serve the steaks with the butter melting on top and the lime wedge on the side. Serves 6.

Shark with Lime Coriander Butter

2 lbs	shark steak, I inch thick and cut into 4 servings	I kg
	olive oil for grilling	
1/4 cup	butter	50 mL
I 1/2 tbsp	fresh coriander, finely chopped	20 mL
2 tsp	fresh lime juice	10 mL
	zest from 1/2 lime	
	salt and freshly ground white pepper	

Mash the butter with a fork until softened a bit. Add the coriander, lime juice and zest, salt and pepper. Combine well. Place on a sheet of waxed paper and form into a log about 1 1/4 inches in diameter. Roll the log tightly in the waxed paper and refrigerate for about twenty minutes. Brush the shark steaks with a little olive oil and grill over hot coals until the interior of the fish is opaque. Unroll the butter and slice into 1/2 inch disks. Serve a disk on top of each shark steak. Serves 4.

Boston Bluefish With Mint Butter

1/3 cup	butter	75 mL
2 tbsp	fresh mint, finely chopped	25 mL
	freshly ground white pepper	
2 lbs	Boston bluefish fillets, cut into 4 servings	1 kg
	olive oil for grilling	
	salt and pepper	
4	lime wedges	4

Combine the mint and white pepper with the butter and blend well. Form into a log about 1 1/4 inches in diameter and roll in wax paper, twisting the ends. Refrigerate for twenty minutes. Brush the grill and the fillets with olive oil. Grill over hot coals, brushing with olive oil occasionally and turning once, until the fillets are opaque throughout. Slice the butter into 1/2 inch disks. Serve the fish with a disk of the mint butter melting on top. Serves 4.

Swordfish with Peaches

1 1/2 - 2 lbs	swordfish, cut about 1 inch thick	750 g - 1 kg
1/2 cup	olive oil	125 mL
3 tbsp	lemon juice	45 mL
1 tbsp	shallots, finely chopped	15 mL
1 tbsp	fresh dill, finely chopped	15 mL
2 tsp	honey	10 mL
2	cloves garlic, peeled and crushed	2
4	freestone peaches, peeled, pitted and cut in half	4

Cut the swordfish into 4 steaks. Combine the marinade ingredients and add the swordfish. Marinate for 1 hour at room temperature. Remove the steaks from the marinade and grill over hot coals, brushing with the marinade and turning once, until the steaks are almost opaque throughout; about 4 or 5 minutes a side. Brush the peach halves with the marinade and grill alongside the swordfish, brushing frequently with the marinade and turning often, until the peaches are nicely glazed on the outside and heated through on the inside. Serves 4.

Tuna with Tomato and Olive Salsa

2 1/2 lbs	tuna steak, 1 inch thick and	1 1/2 kg
	cut into 6 steaks	
	olive oil for grilling	
	salt and pepper	
	tomato and olive salsa (recipe follows)	

Brush the tuna steaks with olive oil, sprinkle with pepper and grill over hot coals until the steaks are browned on the outside but still a little pink in the centre. Sprinkle with salt a few minutes before removing the steaks from the grill. Serve with the salsa on the side. Serves 6.

Tomato and Olive Salsa

2 cups	tomatoes, seeded and chopped	500 mL
1/2 cup	green olives, pitted and chopped	125 mL
1/2 cup	black olives, pitted and chopped	125 mL
2 tbsp	capers, drained	25 mL
3	anchovies, chopped	3
3	garlic cloves, peeled and minced	3
1 tbsp	fresh parsley, finely chopped	15 mL
1/4 cup	olive oil	50 mL
3 tbsp	balsamic vinegar	45 mL

Combine tomatoes, olives, capers, anchovies, garlic, parsley, oil and vinegar and mix well. Let rest for an hour. If made ahead, refrigerate and return to room temperature before serving.

Trout with Almonds

1 - 2 cups	sliced almonds	250 mL - 500 mL
1/4 - 1/2 cup	butter	50 mL - 125 mL
4	whole trout	4
	olive oil for grilling	
	salt and pepper	
4	sprigs of fresh thyme	4
4	sprigs of fresh rosemary	4
4	lemon wedges for garnish	4

Melt butter in medium skillet over moderate heat. Add almonds and sauté until golden brown. Keep warm. Brush the trout with olive oil and stuff the inside with the herbs. Sprinkle with salt and pepper and grill over moderately hot coals, turning once, until browned and cooked through. Serve smothered in almonds with lemon wedges on the side. Serves 4.

Red Snapper with Tomato Olive Salsa

2 lbs	red snapper fillets	I kg
	olive oil for grilling	
	lemon wedges for garnish	
	tomato olive salsa (recipe follows)	

Brush the red snapper with olive oil, sprinkle with salt and pepper and grill over moderately hot coals, turning once, until the fish is cooked through. This will just take a few minutes on each side. Serve with the salsa. Garnish with lemon wedges. Serves 4.

Tomato Olive Salsa

I lb	ripe tomatoes, chopped and seeded	500 g
I/4 cup	basil finely chopped	50 mL
I/2 cup	black olives packed in brine, drained, pitted and chopped	125 mL
I I/2 tbsp	capers, drained	20 mL
I	green onion, green part only, chopped	I
I/2 cup	olive oil	125 mL
	juice of half lemon	
	salt and pepper	

Combine the tomatoes, basil, olives, capers, green onions, olive oil and lemon juice. Season with salt and pepper. Prepare salsa shortly before serving and let sit at room temperature.

Swordfish Steak with Watercress Butter

1/3 cup	butter	75 mL
1	green onion, green part only, finely chopped	1
1/2 cup	watercress leaves, finely cut	125 mL
	dash of hot pepper sauce	
	salt and pepper	
1/2 cup	olive oil	125 mL
2 tsp	green peppercorns, crushed	10 mL
3	garlic cloves, peeled and crushed	3
3 lbs	swordfish steak, about 1 inch thick, cut into 6 steaks	1 1/2 kg

Combine the butter, green onion, watercress, pepper sauce, salt and pepper. Mix and form into a short log, about 1 1/2 inches in diameter, on a sheet of waxed paper. Roll the paper tightly around the log and refrigerate about twenty minutes, until quite firm. Mix together the olive oil, garlic and green peppercorns. Brush the swordfish steaks with the oil mixture and grill over hot coals, about 5 minutes a side, until the fish is opaque. Unwrap the watercress butter and slice into disks about a 1/2 inch thick. Serve the steaks with a disk of the butter melting on top. Serves 6.

Salmon Steak with Guacamole

8	salmon steaks	8
1/2 cup	vegetable oil	125 mL
1/2	jalapeño pepper, seeded and minced	1/2
1/2 tsp	hot sauce	2 mL
1 tbsp	lime juice	15 mL
	guacamole (recipe follows)	

Combine in a dish, the oil, jalapeño pepper, hot sauce and lime juice. Add the salmon and marinate for an hour at room temperature. Grill the salmon over hot coals about 5 minutes per side, until the steaks are opaque throughout. Serve with the guacamole. Serves 8.

Guacamole

1	avocado, at room temperature	2
1	small tomato, seeded and chopped	1
1 tbsp	onion, finely chopped	15 mL
1 tbsp	coriander, finely chopped	15 mL
2 tsp	lime juice	10 mL
	salt and freshly ground pepper	
	hot sauce to taste	

Cut the avocado in half, discard the pit and scoop the pulp into a bowl. Add the tomato, onion, coriander, 2 tsp lime juice, salt and pepper and the hot sauce to taste. Mix well and cover tightly. Keep at room temperature until ready to serve. Refrigerate if serving time is more than a half hour away.

Salmon Fillet with Corn Salsa

	half an Atlantic salmon cut in 1 whole fillet; about 3 lbs (1 1/2 kg)	
1/2 cup	olive oil	125 mL
1/4 to 1/2 tsp	hot sauce	1 to 2 mL

Combine the olive oil and hot pepper sauce. Brush the salmon with the oil mixture and grill over hot coals, skin side up, for about 5 minutes. Turn with two spatulas and grill skin side down until opaque throughout; about 5 more minutes. Remove to a platter and cut into 6 servings. To serve, gently separate the individual serving from the skin and lift it onto each plate. Top with a large spoonful of corn salsa. Serves 6.

Corn Salsa

3	ears of fresh corn	3
1	tomato	1
1	garlic clove, peeled and minced	1
1/2	jalapeño pepper	1/2
1/4	green pepper	1/4
1/4	red pepper	1/4
	juice of 1 lime	
1 tbsp	fresh coriander, finely chopped	15 mL
	few sprigs of parsley, finely chopped	
	generous amount of salt and freshly ground pepper	

Remove husks and silk from the corn and grill over moderately hot coals, brushing with olive oil and turning the cobs every 3 or 4 minutes until lightly browned. Cut the kernels from the cob and place in a bowl. Cut the tomato in half. Remove the seeds, chop into 1/2 inch cubes and add to the corn. Remove the inner membranes and seeds from the peppers, mince the jalapeño and chop the other peppers into 1/2 inch cubes. Add to the corn mixture. Add the garlic, lime juice, coriander, parsley, salt and pepper. Let the mixture sit 30 minutes before serving. If made ahead, chill and return to room temperature before serving.

Uncle Don's Barbecued Salmon

1	whole fresh salmon	1
	butter for grilling	
	lemons	
	salt and freshly ground pepper	

Cut the head and tail from the salmon. Using a sharp fish knife, beginning at the head end and from the belly side, cut the bones, in one long piece from the lower side of the salmon. Flip the fish over and do the same to the other side. With the bones removed, spread the salmon out flat on a buttered piece of foil, spread the salmon with butter, squeeze on some fresh lemon juice, sprinkle with salt and pepper and place over moderately hot coals. Grill without turning until the salmon is opaque throughout. Separate the salmon from the skin while serving. Garnish with lemon wedges. Serves 8 or more, depending on the size of the fish.

Barbecued Smelts

24	little smelts or 12 large smelts	24
1/4 cup	ketjap manis [Indonesian soya sauce]	50 mL
6 tbsp	olive oil	90 mL
1/2 tsp	hot sauce	2 mL
	juice of 1/2 lemon	
4	cloves garlic, crushed	4
1	shallot, minced	1

Combine all the ingredients, but the smelts, and mix well. Add the smelts and marinate for one hour. Grill them over hot coals, brushing with the marinade and turning once, until the smelts are nicely browned and flake easily when pierced with a skewer. Serves 6.

Salmon with Caper Butter

2 tbsp	butter, softened	25 mL
2 tbsp	capers, minced	25 mL
1	large salmon fillet, about 3 lbs (1 1/2 kg)	1
	olive oil for grilling	

Add the capers to the butter and blend well. Place the butter on a square of waxed paper and form into a log about an inch in diameter. Roll the log tightly in the waxed paper and twist the ends. Place in the freezer for 10 minutes or the refrigerator for twenty minutes, or so. Grill the salmon, flesh side down, over moderately hot coals, brushing with the olive oil and turning once, until the outside is browned a little and the inside is opaque; about 5 minutes a side. Unwrap the caper butter and slice into disks. Serve the salmon in sections, separating it from the skin as you go. Place a disk of the butter on each serving. Serves 6.

Whole Stuffed Salmon

I	whole, 4 or 5 lb (2 or 2.2 kg) Salmon, with head, tail and skin intact	I
I	tomato, sliced	I
I	onion, peeled and sliced	I
I	lemon, sliced	I
	olive oil	
	lemon juice	
	salt and pepper	

Have your fishmonger descale the salmon. Clean the fish under cold-running water and dry with paper towels. Brush the inside cavity with olive oil, squeeze on a little lemon juice and sprinkle with salt and pepper. Stuff the cavity with the tomato, onion and lemon slices and, using a darning needle and heavy thread, sew the salmon closed. [If this seems like too much work, just wrap the fish tightly in the foil.] Place the salmon on a large piece of heavy duty foil, brush the salmon with olive oil and wrap it tightly in the foil. Place the salmon over moderately hot coals and grill, turning once, until the inside of the fish is opaque. The conventional rule of thumb is 10 minutes per inch, measured at the thickest part of the fish. Serves about 8 people.

Tuna with Black Olive Salsa

I 1/2 to 2 lbs	tuna steak, cut I 1/4 inches thick	750 g to I kg
1/2 cup	olive oil	125 mL
4	cloves garlic, peeled and crushed	4
1/4 cup	fresh thyme, chopped	50 mL
1/2 tsp	freshly ground black pepper	2 mL
	black olive salsa (recipe follows)	

Combine the olive oil, garlic, thyme and pepper in a dish and add the tuna steak. Marinate at room temperature for about an hour. Combine all ingredients and let sit at room temperature for half an hour. Grill the steak over hot coals, brushing with the marinade and turning once, until the steak is almost opaque. Serve with the black olive salsa. Serves 4.

Black Olive Salsa

I cup	black olives, pitted and chopped	250 mL
2	tomatoes, seeded and chopped	2
I tbsp	olive oil	15 mL
I tbsp	balsamic vinegar	15 mL
I tbsp	shallots, finely chopped	15 mL
2	cloves garlic, minced	2
	salt and freshly ground pepper	

Swordfish Steak with Roasted Pepper Pesto

2 lbs	swordfish steak, cut 1 1/4 inches thick	1 kg
1/2 cup	olive oil	125 mL
1/2 tsp	cayenne pepper	2 mL
1/2 tsp	hot sauce	2 mL
4	lemon wedges	4
	roasted pepper pesto (recipe follows)	

Combine the olive oil, cayenne pepper and hot sauce and pour over the steak. Grill the steak, brushing with the oil and turning once until the outside is browned and the inside is still pink. Serve with the pesto and wedges of lemon. Serves 4.

Roasted Pepper Pesto

3	red bell peppers	3
1	jalapeño pepper	1
3	cloves garlic, peeled and cut in half	3
1/4 cup	fresh basil leaves	50 mL
2 tbsp	olive oil	25 mL
2 tsp	balsamic vinegar	10 mL
	salt and freshly ground pepper	

Roast the peppers over very hot coals until the outer skin is blackened all over. Place the peppers in a paper bag for 5 or 10 minutes to sweat. Remove them from the bag and peel away the outer skin. Cut the peppers open and remove the seeds and inner membranes. Place the peppers in the bowl of a food processor with the garlic, basil, olive oil and vinegar. Process until almost smooth.

Whole Red Snapper

1/2 cup	olive oil	125 mL
1/2 cup	lemon juice	125 mL
	zest of 1 lemon	
1/4 cup	fresh mint leaves, minced	50 mL
2 tbsp	soya sauce	25 mL
4	whole red snappers, scales and fins removed	4

Combine the marinade ingredients in a dish and mix well. Score the fish about 1/8 inch deep and one inch apart in a diagonal pattern on each side of the fish. Marinate the fish for an hour. Grill over hot coals, brushing with the marinade and turning once, about 5 or more minutes a side depending on the thickness of the fish, until the fish flakes easily when pierced with a skewer and the fish is opaque throughout. Serves 4.

Tuna with Orange Butter

4 lbs	tuna steak, cut 1 inch thick	2 kg
	olive oil for grilling	
	salt and freshly ground pepper	
	orange butter (recipe follows)	

Grill the steak over hot coals, brushing with olive oil, sprinkling with salt and freshly ground pepper and turning once, until the steaks are not quite opaque throughout; about 5 minutes a side. Cut the steak into 8 servings. Slice the butter into 1/2 inch disks and serve on top of the steaks. Serves 8.

Orange Butter

	zest of 1 large navel orange	
1/2 cup	butter, softened	125 mL
2 tsp	orange liqueur	10 mL
2 tbsp	freshly squeezed orange juice	25 mL
2 tsp	sugar	10 mL

Combine the orange zest, butter, liqueur, orange juice and sugar, and blend well for a few minutes to combine. Place the mixture on a square of waxed paper and form into a log about 1 1/4" thick. Twist ends. Refrigerate about twenty minutes or more.

Trout with Fresh Herbs

1/4 cup	olive oil	50 mL
3 tbsp	lemon juice	45 mL
	zest of 1 lemon	
	salt and freshly ground pepper	
4	sprigs each of rosemary and thyme	4
4	whole trout	4

Combine olive oil, lemon juice and lemon zest in a dish and add the trout. Marinate about an hour at room temperature. Sprinkle with salt and pepper. Place a sprig of rosemary and a sprig of thyme in each trout. Grill over hot coals, brushing with the marinade and turning once, until the fish are opaque throughout and flake easily when pierced with a skewer; about 4 to 5 minutes a side. Serves 4.

New Social Club Salmon

I	5 lb. (2 1/2 kg) salmon	I
I	lemon, cut in thin slices	I
2 cups	cooked white rice, kept warm	500 mL
I cup	blueberries	250 mL

Rinse the cavity of the salmon and pat it dry. Line the inside of the cavity with the lemon slices. Add the blueberries to the cooked rice and stuff the cavity of the salmon with the mixture. Wrap the fish well with heavy foil, leaving a pencil-size hole at the nose end. Place the salmon over hot coals and cook for a few minutes then reduce the heat to medium. Turn the salmon when steam exits the nose hole. There should be some audible bubbling. Turn the heat up to high for a few minutes, and then reduce again to medium. The total cooking time should be between 20 and 30 minutes. Remove the salmon to a platter and let stand in foil for ten minutes before opening. Remove skin, if it does not come off with the foil, and serve with the rice. Serves 6.

J.C.'s Mayonnaise Salmon on Garlic Mashed Potatoes

I	2 1/2 - 3 lb (I 1/4 - I 1/2 kg) salmon fillet	I
1/4 cup	mayonnaise	50 mL
	garlic mashed potatoes (recipe follows)	

Spread the mayonnaise on a sheet of tin foil. Place the salmon on the foil, skin side down. Grill over hot coals, without turning the salmon, until the flesh is opaque. Spread a portion of potatoes on 4 dinner plates and place a serving of salmon on top. Serves 4.

Garlic Mashed Potatoes

8	medium-sized potatoes, peeled and boiled	8
I tsp	butter	5 mL
2	cloves of garlic, peeled	2
2 tbsp	butter	25 mL
	cream to taste	

Mash the potatoes. Sauté the garlic lightly in the tsp of butter. Remove from the heat and mash with the blade of a knife. Blend the mashed garlic with 2 tbsp of butter and add to the potatoes. Add cream and stir until the desired consistency is reached.

SEAFOOD

Ginger Shrimp

I I/2 lbs	raw shrimp	750 g
I/4 cup	balsamic vinegar	50 mL
3 tbsp	soya sauce	45 mL
I/4 cup	olive oil	50 mL
2	cloves garlic, peeled and crushed	2
2 tsp	fresh ginger, peeled and grated	I0 mL
2 tsp	honey	I0 mL
	dash hot pepper sauce	

Peel and devein the shrimp, but leave the tails on. Combine all ingredients and marinate for an hour. Brush the grill with olive oil and grill a few minutes a side until the shrimp curl and turn pink. Serves 6 as an appetizer.

Shrimp and Scallops with Yellow or Red Vegetables

18	large sea scallops	18
12	large shrimps	12
12	yellow or red cherry tomatoes	12
12	shitake mushrooms	12
1	yellow or red pepper, seeds removed and cut into 1 1/2 inch pieces	1
	salt and pepper	
1/4 cup	olive oil	50 mL
2 tbsp	balsamic vinegar	25 mL
6	lemon wedges	6

Thread 3 scallops, 2 shrimps, 2 tomatoes, 2 mushrooms and a couple of pieces of pepper alternately on each of 6 skewers. Combine the olive oil, balsamic vinegar and thyme in a small bowl and brush the skewers with the mixture. Place the skewers on the grill over very hot coals, and grill a few minutes a side, brushing with the oil mixture and turning until the shrimp are pink and the scallops are opaque throughout. Serves 6.

Mussels with Four Pepper Salsa

1	red pepper	1
1	green pepper	1
2	jalapeño peppers	2
1	small hot red pepper	1
1/4 cup	fresh cilantro, finely chopped	50 mL
1/4 cup	olive oil	50 mL
2 tbsp	white wine vinegar	25 mL
	salt and pepper	
24	mussels plus a few extras in case of spoilage	24

Seed and finely chop all the peppers. Mix in a bowl with the cilantro, olive oil, vinegar, salt and pepper. Put 1/2 of the mixture in the bowl of a food processor and process a few seconds until a fine grain is obtained. Add this mixture to the remaining salsa. Scrub and rinse the mussels. Place them over hot coals and grill until they open wide. Discard any mussels that do not open wide. Remove the mussels to a platter. Break off and discard the shells that the mussels are not attached to. Loosen the mussel in its shell and spoon a little salsa into the shell. Serves 6 as an appetizer.

Seafood Pasta

2	fresh lobsters	2
I dozen	large sea scallops	I dozen
2 dozen	mussels	2 dozen
	olive oil for grilling	
1/4 cup	olive oil	50 mL
4	garlic cloves, crushed	4
2 28 oz	cans Italian plum tomatoes	?
I tbsp	fresh basil, finely cut	15 mL
	lemon wedges for garnish	
	spaghetti	

Kill the lobsters either by inserting the tip of a sharp knife into the cross on their backs behind their head or by plunging them into boiling water for a minute or so. Place the lobsters on the grill over medium hot coals and cook about 10 minutes until the meat inside is opaque. Turn the lobsters occasionally to keep the shells from burning. Remove them to a platter and keep them warm. Place the mussels over high heat and cook until the shells open. Remove and cover to keep warm. Brush the scallops with olive oil and grill over hot coals until the outside is browned but the inside is not quite opaque, turning once. Meanwhile, heat the 1/4 cup of olive oil over moderate heat and add the garlic. Cook until softened but not brown. Add the tomatoes and basil and stir to heat for a few minutes.

Cook the spaghetti in boiling water until cooked through, but still firm. Drain the pasta and place on a serving platter. Break the claws and tails away from the body of the lobsters. Reserve the bodies for another use. With a sharp knife, cut a slit down the middle of the underside of the tails and smash the claws so that the meat is easier to remove from the shells. Arrange the lobster pieces and other seafood on top of the pasta. Pour the tomato sauce over all and bring to the table. Toss a little at the table and serve. Serves 4.

Oysters with Barbecue Butter

24	oysters	24
1/2 cup	butter, softened	125 mL
1 tbsp	lemon juice	15 mL
1/4	red pepper, seeded and minced	1/4
1/4	green pepper, seeded and minced	1/4
3 tbsp	bottled or homemade barbecue sauce	45 mL
2 tbsp	fresh parsley, chopped	25 mL
	freshly ground black pepper	
1	lemon	1

Shuck the oysters. Separate the oyster from the shell and place on the cup-shaped half shell. In a bowl, combine the butter, lemon juice, peppers, barbecue sauce, parsley and black pepper. Mix well and spoon a little onto each oyster. Grill the oysters over very hot coals until the edges of the oyster begin to curl. Cut the lemon in wedges and serve with the oysters. Serves 4.

Lobsters Grilled with Lemon Butter

4	live lobsters	4
3/4 cup	butter	175 mL
	juice of 2 lemons	

Plunge the lobsters briefly into boiling water, one at a time, to kill them. With a mallet, smash the claws just enough to crack the shell and inner membrane and, with a sharp knife, cut a long slit down the middle of the underside of the tail. Melt the butter and add the lemon juice. Grill the whole lobsters over moderately hot coals, brushing with the lemon butter and turning, until the lobster meat inside is opaque. Serve with more lemon butter for dipping. Serves 4.

Garlic Lemon Shrimp

16	extra large, black tiger shrimp	16
1/2 cup	olive oil	125 mL
1/4 cup	lemon juice	50 mL
3 or 4	garlic cloves, peeled and crushed	3 or 4
	salt and pepper	

Mix the olive oil, lemon juice, garlic, salt and pepper together in a small bowl. Shell and devein the shrimp, leaving the tails intact. Dip the shrimp in the oil mixture and place on a grill over hot coals. Brush the shrimp frequently with the oil and grill 3 or 4 minutes, turning once, until the shrimp have turned pink and are opaque throughout. Serves 4.

Mussels with
Watercress Butter

If the following method seems like too much work for you, which it could be if you are serving a crowd, throw all the mussels into a grill basket and cook over hot coals until the shells open. Serve them on a platter with a bowl of melted watercress butter. For a variation, you can substitute garlic butter [which I confess I am nuts about], or melted butter with lime juice [another addiction]. If you are serving a large number of people, you could even opt for all three.

24	mussels, debearded	24
1/4 cup	butter, softened	50 mL
1/4 cup	watercress leaves, minced	50 mL

To remove sand from the mussels, soak them in a bowl of cold water for several minutes. Lift the mussels out and check the bowl for sand. Repeat the process until the sand is gone. To hasten this procedure, you can add a little flour to the water.

Combine the watercress and butter in a little bowl. Place the mussels on the grill over hot coals and grill until they open. Break off the half shell that the mussel is not attached to and set the mussel back on the grill in the grooves provided between the bars of the grill. Place 1/4 teaspoon of the watercress butter on top of the mussel and grill about one minute more. Serves 4 as an hors d'oeuvre.

Scallops with Mangos and Limes

This dish does not have to be grilled on skewers. If the scallops are nice and big, they can be put straight on the grill with big wedges of mango and lime. The trick is to cook them quickly over high heat so that the inside doesn't cook too much before the scallops brown on the outside.

I	mango	I
I/4 cup	olive oil	50 mL
	white pepper	
	juice and zest of I lime	
I I/2 lbs	sea scallops	750 g
I	lime, cut in 8 wedges	

Soak 8 wooden skewers in water for I hour. Cut the mango into chunks roughly the size of the scallops. Cut the shape on the mango through to the pit and then cut the chunk away from the pit. Do not remove the outer skin until after you separate the flesh from the pit. Combine the olive oil, white pepper, lime zest and juice in a small dish. Thread the mangos and scallops equally on the 8 skewers. End with a wedge of lime on each skewer. Grill over very hot coals, brushing with the marinade and turning as needed to keep the scallops from browning too heavily. Grill until the outside of the scallops is nicely browned and the inside is just cooked through. When eating, squeeze the lime wedge over the scallops and mangos. Serves 4.

VEGETABLES

Sweet Potatoes

3	large sweet potatoes	3
	olive oil for grilling	
	salt and pepper	

Slice the unpeeled sweet potatoes into slices; about 1/4 inch thick. Brush them with olive oil and grill over moderately hot coals, turning two or three times and brushing with the oil, until they are crispy and browned on the outside and tender inside. In the last few minutes of grilling, sprinkle them with salt and pepper. Serves 6.

Grill-Baked Potatoes

The use of skewers in this recipe can decrease the cooking time of the potatoes by about 10 or 15 minutes. It will do the same thing in your oven as well. Like oven-baked potatoes, they can be served with a variety of topping; melted butter, roasted garlic olive oil, sour cream and chives, crème fraîche and mashed roasted garlic, grated cheddar cheese, etc.

4 6 oz	baking potatoes	4 175 g

Scrub potatoes and place on metal skewers. Even if the skewers are long enough, you can't put more than one potato on each one. Place potatoes over moderately hot coals and grill, turning occasionally, for about 45 minutes or until tender. For a softer skin the potatoes can be brushed with a little olive oil or butter while grilling. Serves 4.

Grilled Baby Pattypan Squash

18	small whole pattypan squash	18
1/3 cup	white wine vinegar	75 mL
1/2 cup	olive oil	125 mL
1/2 tsp	Dijon mustard	2 mL
	salt and pepper	

Combine vinegar, oil, mustard, salt and pepper. Put the squash over hot coals and brush with the vinaigrette. Grill, turning frequently, until brown on all sides and tender inside. Serves 6.

Corn on the Cob in the Husk

6	ears of corn	6
1/4 cup	butter	50 mL

Peel the husks from the corn leaving the husks attached to the cob at the base. Remove the silk. Plunge the corn cobs into cold water for about five minutes and then rinse. Melt the butter. Pat the corn cobs dry and brush with the melted butter. Pull the husks back into place. Put them over moderately hot coals and grill about 15 minutes, turning occasionally. Serves 6.

Baby Beets and Carrots

18	baby beets with greens	18
1 1/2 lbs	baby carrots with greens	750 g
1/2 cup	olive oil	125 mL
	few sprigs of rosemary	

Cut the greens from the beets and carrots, leaving about an inch of stem on the vegetables. Boil the beets in water about 5 minutes. Boil the carrots about 3 minutes. Peel the outer skin off the beets. The vegetables can be prepared ahead to this point and refrigerated until ready to grill. Remove the leaves from the rosemary sprigs and place in a small saucepan with the olive oil. Heat the oil for a few minutes until it is quite hot. Cool. Brush the vegetables with the olive oil and grill over moderately hot coals, brushing with the oil and turning, until brown on all sides. A grilling rack should be used if the vegetables are too small for your barbecue grill. If you don't have a grill rack, skewer the vegetables. Serves 6.

Cathy's Pepper Potatoes

24	small new potatoes	24
1/4 cup	President's Choice 4 Peppercorn Steak Spice	50 mL
1/4 - 1/2 cup olive oil		50 mL - 125 mL

Place the potatoes on a piece of foil with the edges crimped up. Sprinkle the potatoes liberally with olive oil and steak spice. Set the foil containers on the grill over hot coals and grill, turning as needed, until the potatoes are browned on all sides, and tender when pierced with a skewer, about 40 minutes. Serves 8.

Vegetable Packages

1	large head of green or red cabbage	1
1	leek	1
3	cobs of corn, husks and silk removed	3
2	jalapeño peppers	2
1	red pepper	1
6	green onions, trimmed of roots and 2 inches of top leaves	6
	olive oil for grilling	
	salt and pepper	

Remove the core from the cabbage by cutting it at a 45 degree angle about 2 1/2 inches deep. Place cabbage in a large pot and cover with boiling water. Cover the pot with a lid or an inverted bowl and let sit 5 to 10 minutes. Remove 6 leaves. Repeat the process if necessary. If the inner leaves are too stiff to manipulate, try boiling them briefly in water. Refresh the leaves under cold water and set aside. Remove the leek leaves from the stock by slitting the base of the leaf and peeling it away from the stalk. Place in a dish and cover with boiling water. Let sit for about a minute. Remove and refresh under cold water and cut into ribbons about 1/4 inch wide. Set aside. Grill the corn over moderately hot coals, brushing with olive oil and turning, until the corn browns a little on all sides. Cut the kernels from the cob and place in a bowl. Grill the peppers over hot coals until the outer skin is blackened on all sides. Remove the peppers to a paper bag and close tightly. Let sit for 10 minutes to steam. Peel the outer skin from the peppers, cut open, remove seeds, chop the pepper and mince the jalapeños. Add to the corn. Grill the green onions over moderately hot coals, brushing with the olive oil and turning frequently, until lightly browned. This will only take a few minutes. Chop the green onions and add to the corn mixture. Season with salt and pepper.

Divide the mixture into 6 portions. Trim away the stiff outer edge of the cabbage core. Place a portion of the corn mixture in the centre of each leaf. Fold the core edge over, then the opposite edge and repeat with the other two edges, forming a little package. Tie the length of the package with one leek ribbon and the width with another ribbon. Trim away left over ties. Refrigerate until ready to cook. Grill over moderately hot coals, brushing with olive oil and turning once, until browned on the outside and heated through on the inside. Serves 6.

Orange Glazed Carrots

12	carrots, peeled and cut in half lengthwise	12
1/4 cup	vegetable oil	50 mL
2 tbsp	brown sugar	25 mL
1/2 tsp	cardamon	2 mL
1 tsp	grated orange zest	5 mL
1 tsp	fresh ginger, peeled and grated	5 mL
1 tbsp	fresh orange juice	15 mL

Combine everything but the carrots in a small bowl. Brush the carrots with the oil mixture and grill over moderately hot coals, brushing with the marinade and turning as needed until the carrots are nicely glazed on the outside and tender but crisp on the inside. Serves 8.

Garlic Corn on the Cob

12	ears of corn	12
	olive oil or olive oil with garlic essence for grilling	
	salt	

Remove the husks and silk from the corn, brush with the olive oil and grill over moderately hot coals on about 4 sides of the corn, for about 3 minutes or so a side, until the corn is browned a little on all sides. Brush the top side of the corn with the oil and sprinkle with salt as you grill. Serves 6.

Curried Butternut Squash

1	butternut squash with a long neck	1
1 tbsp	curry powder	15 mL
1/4 cup	olive oil	50 mL

Leaving the skin on, slice the neck of the squash into 1/2 inch slices. Reserve the rest of the squash for another use. Combine the olive oil and curry powder. Brush it on the slices of squash and grill over moderately hot coals, brushing with the oil mixture and turning as needed to prevent burning, until the squash is nicely browned on the outside and tender on the inside. Serves 4 to 8 depending on the size of the neck of the squash.

Basil Grilled Broccoli

1/4 cup	olive oil	50 mL
1	clove garlic, peeled and minced	1
1/4 cup	fresh basil leaves, finely chopped	50 mL
	salt and freshly ground pepper	
4	stalks of broccoli	4

Combine the olive oil, garlic, basil, salt and pepper and mix well. Trim an inch or two from the stems of the broccoli and cut the stalks in half lengthwise. Brush them all over with the oil mixture. Grill over moderately hot coals, brushing with the oil and turning as needed to prevent over browning, until the broccoli stalk is tender. Serves 4.

Avocados with Garlic and Lemon

1	avocado	1
2 tbsp	olive oil	25 mL
1	clove garlic, peeled and mashed	1
4	wedges of lemon	4

Combine the garlic and oil in a little dish. Cut the avocado into quarters and remove from the pit. Peel the outer skin away from the avocado and brush with the oil. Grill over hot coals, turning frequently until the outside of the avocado is nicely browned. Serve with lemon. Serves 4.

DESSERT

Peaches with Raspberries

6	peaches, preferably freestone, peeled, halved and pitted	6
I cup	fresh or frozen raspberries	250 mL
3 tbsp	fruit-powdered sugar	45 mL
I tbsp	lemon juice	15 mL
I cup	whipping cream, whipped	250 mL
I tbsp	confectioner's sugar	15 mL
I tsp	vanilla	5 mL
24 to 36	fresh, whole raspberries for garnish vegetable or almond oil for grilling	24 to 36

Mash the berries through a sieve and discard the seeds. Add the sugar and lemon juice. Stir until well-combined. Grill the peaches over moderately hot coals, brushing with vegetable oil and turning as needed, until the peaches are heated through and are glazed a little on the outside. Add the sugar and vanilla to whipped cream. Pour the raspberry purée onto 6 plates. Place a peach half slightly off-centre in the pool of purée. Place the other peach half partially overlapping the first one. Garnish each plate with a dollop of whipped cream and a scattering of fresh whole berries. Serves 6.

Pears with Plum Sauce

3	purple plums, cut into quarters, pitted	3
1/3 cup	water	75 mL
3 tbsp	sugar	45 mL
1/4 tsp	cinnamon	1 mL
3	large pears, halved, cored	3
1/4 cup	vegetable oil	50 mL
1 tsp	sugar	5 mL
	vanilla ice cream or frozen yogurt	
6	sprigs of mint for garnish	6

Place the plums in a saucepan with the water, sugar and cinnamon and bring to a boil. Reduce the heat and simmer about 15 minutes until the fruit has blended with the water, but the sauce is still quite liquid. Strain the liquid and cool. Peel the pears, core and cut into halves. Combine the vegetable oil and sugar and brush the pear halves with it. Grill over moderate coals, brushing with the sweetened oil and turning until the pears are heated through and golden on the outside. Place a scoop of vanilla ice cream or frozen yogurt on six plates. Lean a pear half against each scoop and pour the plum sauce over the pear trying to keep it away from the ice cream. Garnish with mint. Serves 6.

Caramel Banana Crêpes

1 cup	brown sugar	250 mL
1/3 cup	water	75 mL
1/4 cup	butter	50 mL
6	small bananas	6
	dark rum	
1 cup	whipping cream, whipped	250 mL
1 tbsp	confectioner's sugar	15 mL
1 tsp	vanilla	5 mL
6	dessert crêpes	6

Combine the 1 cup of brown sugar with the water and butter in a medium saucepan and bring to a boil over high heat, stirring until the sugar dissolves. Simmer over moderate heat until the sauce becomes syrupy [about 15 minutes]. Cut a slit in the skin of each banana, along the inner curve of the fruit. Place a few drops of dark rum in each slit. Grill the banana over moderately hot coals, turning several times, until the banana is heated through. Add the confectioner's sugar and vanilla to the whipped cream. Cut the stem of the banana and remove the peel. Roll the grilled bananas in the crêpes and place on six plates. Pour the caramel sauce over each crêpe and add a dollop of whipped cream on the side. Serves 6.

Meringues with Tropical Fruit and Passion Fruit Caramel Sauce

Do not attempt to make meringues on a humid day. They will drive you crazy. The best way to make them is to wait until you won't need your oven for about eight hours. When you are finished baking them, turn the oven to its lowest setting and let them sit in the oven to dry completely. They simply dissolve in your mouth.

Ripe passion fruit can be difficult to find. Don't let the lack of a good passion fruit stand between you and this dessert. Substitute freshly squeezed orange juice. It will be wonderful on the tropical fruit.

4	egg whites	4
1/2 cup	sugar	125 mL
3/4 cup	icing sugar	175 mL
1 cup	whipping cream	250 mL
1 tbsp	icing sugar	15 mL
1 tsp	vanilla	5 mL
1	pineapple	1
1	papaya	1
1	mango	1
1 tbsp	honey	15 mL
1/3 cup	vegetable oil	75 mL

Combine the sugar and icing sugar in a small bowl and mix well. Put the egg whites in the large bowl of an electric mixer and beat them until soft peaks have formed. Add a little of the sugar and beat until stiff peaks have formed. Gently fold in the rest of the combined sugars. Butter and flour a baking sheet. Make six or more round serving size disks with the meringue, spreading them with a metal spatula so they are relatively the same thickness. Bake in a 250°F oven for 70 to 80 minutes until the meringues are lightly browned and completely dry.

Whip the cream and fold in the icing sugar and vanilla. Refrigerate until ready to serve. Cut the outer skin from the pineapple, papaya and mango. Cut the fruit into long wedges. Stir the honey into the vegetable oil and brush the fruit with it. Grill the fruit over moderately hot coals, brushing with the oil and turning, until the fruit is heated through and browned a little on the outside. Place a meringue on 6 individual plates. Put a dollop of whipped cream on each meringue. Place a wedge of each fruit on top, cutting the fruit into shorter wedges if necessary. Pour the passion fruit caramel sauce over all. Serves 6.

Fruit Caramel Sauce

1 cup	brown sugar	250 mL
1 or 2	passion fruits	1 or 2
1/4 cup	butter	50 mL

Cut the passion fruit in half. Scoop out the pulp and seeds into a sieve set over a bowl. Press the seeds and pulp with the back of a spoon to get about 1/2 cup of juice and pulp. Put the measured fruit in a medium saucepan with the brown sugar and butter. Place over medium heat and stir until the sugar dissolves. Increase heat and boil the mixture until the sauce is reduced to about 1 cup. Keep warm.

Caramel Mangos with Ice Cream and Almonds

I	mango, cut in wedges and peeled	I
1/4 cup	almond oil	50 mL
I tbsp	honey	15 mL
I tbsp	lime juice	15 mL
2/3 cup	almonds, slivered and toasted	150 mL
	container of vanilla ice cream	
	caramel sauce (recipe follows)	

Combine the almond oil, honey and lime juice. Brush the mango wedges with the mixture and grill over moderately hot coals until the mangos are golden brown. Serve over ice cream with the caramel sauce and toasted almonds. Serves 6.

The almonds are toasted in a 400°F oven for 5 minutes or so, until they turn a golden brown. Watch them carefully; they can burn very quickly.

Caramel Sauce

I cup	brown sugar	250 mL
1/2 cup	lime juice	125 mL
1/4 cup	butter	50 mL

Combine the brown sugar, 1/2 cup lime juice and butter in a small saucepan over medium heat, stirring until the sugar is dissolved. Increase the heat and cook until the sauce is reduced, but still a little runny. Keep warm.

Apples with Dried Cherries and Maple Sauce

4	Dudley apples, peeled, cored and quartered	4
3/4 cup	dried cherries	175 mL
3 tbsp	brandy	45 mL
1/2 cup	brown sugar	125 mL
1/2 cup	maple syrup	125 mL
1/4 cup	butter	50 mL
1/4 cup	lemon juice	50 mL
1 tsp	cinnamon	5 mL
2 tbsp	brown sugar	25 mL
	vanilla ice cream or vanilla frozen yogurt	

Pour the brandy over the cherries in a small bowl. Let stand for half an hour. Combine the 1/2 cup brown sugar, maple syrup and butter in a medium saucepan and heat over moderate heat, stirring until the sugar dissolves and the mixture comes to a boil. Cook for 10 minutes or so, stirring occasionally until the mixture thickens somewhat. Add the brandy from the cherries and cook again until the mixture is thickened again.

Brush the apples with a mixture of the lemon juice, cinnamon and the 2 tbsp of brown sugar and grill over moderately hot coals, brushing with the lemon mixture and turning as needed, until the apples are glazed and tender, but still firm.

Add the cherries to the sauce and let stand for a minute off the heat. Place a scoop of the ice cream or frozen yogurt onto each of 4 separate dessert plates or compote glasses. Place the grilled apples on top. Spoon the caramel sauce and cherries over all. Serves 4.

Tropical Fruit with Puff Pastry and Pineapple Caramel Sauce

	1 package of frozen puff pastry, defrosted	
1	fresh pineapple	1
1	fresh starfruit	1
1	fresh mango	1
1/3 cup	peanut oil	75 mL
1 tbsp	brown sugar	15 mL
1 cup	whipping cream, whipped	250 mL
1/2 tsp	vanilla	2 mL
1 tbsp	confectioner's sugar	15 mL
8	sprigs fresh mint for garnish	8
	pineapple caramel sauce (recipe follows)	

Roll out the pastry until it is 1/8 inch thick. Cut out 8 circles about 3" in diameter or several shapes per serving or 8 palm trees, fit them closely together on the rolled pastry. This can be done in a primitive free-hand style or you can make a cardboard template to use as a guide. Place the shapes on an ungreased cookie sheet, spray with water and bake in a preheated 400°F oven for 7 to 10 minutes until they puff up and turn a light golden brown. If the dough becomes too soft while doing this, chill the palm trees before baking them.

Cut the outer skin from the pineapple and cut into 8 wedges, cutting away the hard inner core from each wedge. Cut sections from the mango and cut away outer skin from each wedge. Slice the starfruit into 1/2 inch slices. Combine the peanut oil with the tablespoon of brown sugar. Brush the fruit with the oil mixture and grill over moderately hot coals, turning and brushing with the oil, until golden on the outside and heated through on the inside.

Add the vanilla and sugar to the whipped cream and mix well. Pour a pool of pineapple caramel sauce on 8 dessert plates. Place a serving of puff pastry on each plate. Add a dollop of whipped cream. Lay pieces of grilled fruit on top, garnish with sprigs of fresh mint and serve. Serves 8.

Pineapple Caramel Sauce

2 cups	brown sugar	500 mL
1/2 cup	butter	125 mL
1/2 cup	pineapple juice	125 mL

Combine the brown sugar, butter and pineapple juice in a medium saucepan and bring to a boil over moderate heat, stirring until the sugar dissolves. Continue to cook until the mixture thickens a little. Keep warm.

Pears Cloaked in Chocolate with Crème Anglaise

6	pears, peeled, halved and cored	6
2 tbsp	lime juice	25 mL
I tbsp	brown sugar	15 mL
8 ozs	chocolate, melted	250 g
I tsp	butter	5 mL
6	sprigs of fresh mint	6
	crème anglaise (recipe follows)	

Combine the lime juice and brown sugar. Brush the pear halves with the lime juice mixture and grill over moderately hot coals, turning and brushing with the marinade as needed, until the outside is glazed a golden brown and the inside is heated through. Cool.

Add the butter to the melted chocolate and, using two forks, dip the pears one at a time in the chocolate. Let the excess chocolate drip back into the bowl and then set the dipped pears on waxed paper, core side down, to cool. Pour a pool of crème anglaise onto 6 dessert plates. Place 2 cloaked pears on each plate. Garnish with fresh mint. Serves 6.

Crème Anglaise

1 1/4 cups	milk	300 mL
1/2 cup	whipping cream	125 mL
1	vanilla bean	1
1/3 cup	sugar	75 mL
4	large egg yolks	4
2 tsp	cornstarch	10 mL

Combine the milk, cream and vanilla bean in a medium saucepan over high heat and bring quickly to a boil. Let sit for 10 minutes. Beat the eggs and sugar together with a whisk, until the mixture turns a pale yellow and forms a ribbon when the whisk is lifted from the bowl. Fold in the cornstarch. Remove the vanilla bean from the milk mixture and stir a little of the milk into the egg mixture. Pour this back into the saucepan with the milk mixture and cook, stirring constantly with a wooden spoon, until the crème is thickened and coats the spoon when lifted from the saucepan. This will take about 20 minutes. Pour the sauce into a bowl and cover tightly with plastic wrap. Chill in the refrigerator.

DRINKS

The Woodstock Piña Colada

I cup	unsweetened pineapple juice	250 mL
1/2 cup	dark rum	125 mL
1/4 cup	coconut cream	50 mL
2 cups	crushed ice	500 mL
2	large wedges of fresh pineapple	2

Combine the juice, rum, coconut cream and ice in a blender at high speed for about 30 seconds, until the mixture is slushy. Pour into chilled glasses. Garnish with wedges of pineapple. Serves 2.

Margaritas

I cup	lime juice	250 mL
I cup	tequila	250 mL
1/2 cup	Cointreau	125 mL
1/4 cup	sugar	50 mL
	crushed ice	
	salt	
	several limes	

Combine the lime juice, tequila, Cointreau and sugar in a blender with enough ice to make a slush. Moisten the rim of four glasses with a wedge of lime and invert the glass onto a dish of salt. Add the margarita mixture to the glass and squeeze a wedge of lime over the drink. Throw the spent lime into the drink and serve. Serves 4.

Fuzzy Navels

3 cups	fresh orange juice	750 mL
I cup	peach schnapps	250 mL
I	peach, peeled and cut into 8 wedges	I
2	thick orange slices, cut in half	2
	ice cubes	

Combine the orange juice and schnapps and mix well. Put ice cubes into four frosted glasses and add the orange mixture. Garnish with a wedge of peach and a half slice of orange. Serves 4.

Strawberry Lemon Slush

2 cups	fresh strawberries, stems removed	500 mL
I cup	sugar	250 mL
3 cups	water, divided	750 mL
I cup	fresh lemon juice	250 mL
	crushed ice	
4	large strawberries with the stems intact for garnish	4
4	wedges of lemon for garnish	4

Purée the strawberries in a blender. Combine the sugar, I cup of the water and the lemon juice. Stir until the sugar has dissolved. Add the other 2 cups of water and the puréed strawberries and combine well. Pour into glasses of crushed ice and add a whole strawberry and a wedge of lemon for garnish. Serves 4.

Carey's White Wine Sangria

2	limes	2
I	orange	I
I	lemon	I
I	nectarine or peach	I
I/2 cup	sugar	125 mL
I/2 cup	orange liqueur	125 mL
I/2 cup	brandy	125 mL
	2 750 ml bottles of dry white wine	
	I 750 ml bottle of soda water	
	ice cubes	

Cut the fruit into wedges or slices and place in a very large pitcher. Add the sugar, liqueur, brandy and wine and stir well. Cover and refrigerate for about 4 hours. Just before serving, add lots of ice and the soda water to the pitcher. Serves 12.

Bev's Bellini Slush

I	bottle sparkling white wine	I
4-6	ripe peaches, peeled and chopped	4-6
	juice of 2 limes	
2 tbsp	Grand Marnier or Crème de Cassis	25 mL

Put the peaches, lime juice and liqueur in the bowl of a food processor and purée. Pour into a pitcher with the wine and freeze 15 minutes or until ice crystals form. Pour into glasses. Serves 6 to 8 people.

BROILMASTER®

A Division of Martin Industries

P.O. Box 128
Florence, Al; 35631

1-205-767-0330

*For more copies of this cookbook
please write to the address above.*

Printed in U.S.A.